ALL
YOU
CAN
BE

ALL
YOU
CAN
BE

Thomas Ervin

*An Action Plan
for Real Estate
Sales Success*

PRENTICE HALL PRESS • NEW YORK

Published by Prentice Hall Press
A Division of Simon & Schuster, Inc.
Gulf + Western Building
One Gulf + Western Plaza
New York, NY 10023

PRENTICE HALL PRESS is a trademark of Simon & Schuster, Inc.

Library of Congress No. 86-61052

Manufactured in the United States of America

ISBN: 0-13-022567-3

10   9   8   7   6   5   4   3   2   1

First Edition

To DOROTHY WERNER,
For Her Faith and Valuable Insights

CONTENTS

THE EAGLE AND THE HAWK

by John Denver

I am the eagle
I live in high country
In rocky cathedrals
That reach to the sky

I am the hawk
And there's love on my feathers
The time is still turning
They soon will be dry

And all who see me
And all who believe in me
Share in the freedom
I feel when I fly

Come dance with the west winds
In touch on the mountaintops
Sail on a canyon
And on to the stars

And reach for the heavens
And hope for the future
And all that we can be
Not what we are

Note: This song reprinted with permission of John Denver.

PREFACE

Realizing every financial goal you have ever had is possible in the pursuit of a real estate career. However, it doesn't just happen. You have to make it happen. This book has been designed, page by page, to help you gain the necessary insights into the mental attitude of the people at the top of their profession.

We will accomplish this by examining the role you must play in your own success. Through exhaustive personal interviews with the top earners in our business, we have been privileged to learn about their individual success stories.

Afterward we will pull everything together to see how our newly gained knowledge applies to your own future.

Before we begin I want to point out that you will not profit from reading this book unless you decide to change the way you perceive yourself and your potential. We all have spent many years designing self-imposed limits. These self-imposed limits often prevent us from ever reaching the fulfillment of our dreams.

We will enable you to remove these limits by seeing the extraordinary achievements of people like you and me. We will learn from an 18-year-old woman in California and a 66-year-old grandmother in Michigan and many others who have made it big in their own unique way.

John Denver's song "The Eagle and the Hawk" epitomizes the deepest yearnings of a committed, self-improving, top-producing salesperson. Let's take a few lines from this song and see how it applies to you.

I live in high country . . . Do you identify with winners? Do you have a good self-image? All top producers live in high country. They visualize themselves as being among the top people in their field. With this vision clearly stated, they then strive with every fiber within them to fulfill the successful vision they have of themselves. Regardless of disappointments and frustrations in your past life, envision yourself as becoming a huge success in real estate sales.

. . . *the freedom I feel when I fly.* Are you flying? Is your life exciting and rewarding? Do you feel good about your accomplishments? All top producers have been able to build a momentum into their lives that continues to enhance further growth and fulfillment. They are on a roll. Success builds confidence. With more confidence, you dare to do things that you were afraid to do in the past. You then gain new successes that, in turn, give you greater confidence to stretch further. Around and around the circle goes, picking up in speed and excitement with each revolution. Your circle will never begin spinning unless and until you make a decision to "go for it!"

And reach for the heavens . . . What are you reaching for? Do you have a goal? Is it a general goal, such as you want someday to be rich or is it a specifc goal, such as you want to be earning $100,000 per year by age 35? Most top producers know what they want and how they are going to get what they want. Some people write their goals down on a piece of paper and carry it around in their wallet or purse. Others put goals down on a paper that is sealed in an envelope to be opened on a certain date.

The personal goals for most salespeople are usually broken down into four categories:

- Financial Goal—I want to earn *$50,000* a year.
- Volume Goal—I want to sell *$5 million* a year in volume.
- Ranking Goal—I want to be the *top person* in my office.
- Material Goal—I want to buy a *Cadillac* with my earnings.

State clearly and simply what your personal goal is. It will help you focus your energies around a central theme. With a goal in mind, you will be better able to use this book to design your own personal game plan to reach your goal.

And hope for the future . . . Are you an optimistic person? Is your glass half full or half empty? All top producers believe that good things will happen if they apply themselves. You must have or begin to develop a "can do" attitude to sustain you through the rough times that all successful people face on the way to the top.

And all that we can be, not what we are. Are you satisfied with yourself? Do you think you are through growing as a person? All top producers are constantly challenging themselves to learn new things and try new ideas. To paraphrase Tennyson's line, "'Tis better to have tried and lost, than never to have tried at all." Top producers do lose sometimes, but they keep coming back again and again until they have become winners. They never give up on themselves. These experiences help them discover that great reservoir of human strength and vitality that we all possess.

On the following pages, keep an open mind to the concepts and stories you read. Your tendency may be to tell yourself that you couldn't do this, or that a certain technique is not your style. Although this may be true, please don't be too hasty to make judgments until you have finished work on the all-important final chapter.

**ALL
YOU
CAN
BE**

The Original Drummer

I know I would have liked him, this Merit Welton. He was a salesman who dared to be different. Unshackled by custom and tradition, he set an example for free-spirited people who believe in themselves and their ability to determine their own destiny.

In 1832, most of rural America bought all the necessities of life from the local general store. The general store owners kept their stock up by ordering through catalogs and from one or two buying trips each year. These buying trips were made to one of the major trading centers such as New Orleans. Here they saw the sights, bought merchandise, and returned home well stocked with all the latest stories and a wagon loaded with treasures from the Orient, Europe, and places unknown.

Salespersons who represented the wholesalers and traders would linger around hotel lobbies waiting for the country gentlemen to check in. A tip to a bellhop or desk clerk would reveal the identity and hometown of each traveler. Free tickets, dinner, and many other big-city pleasures were offered to draw patronage away from a competitor.

Merit Welton was a button salesman with the Scovil Manufacturing Company of Waterbury, Connecticut. He, too, was one of those salespeople hanging around the hotels waiting for the customers to show up. For some reason he got fed up with this routine and decided to do the two things that every great salesperson must do:

1. Do something other salespeople are not willing to do.
2. Provide additional service for your customer.

Rather than fighting it out in hotel lobbies with every salesman of every other company, he decided to go to his customers. After packing his horse with button samples, he set out through the Midwest in the summer of 1832. I am sure many store owners were shocked at the sight of this dapper salesman walking into their store with his button samples attractively displayed in his felt-lined display case.

He showed ingenuity and imagination by providing a service his competition did not offer. He was the first traveling salesman in America. Can you imagine the huge volume of orders he received by bringing his samples to the customer, whose closest competitor was hundreds of miles away? Can you envision what this service meant to these store owners?

It was not the quality and pricing of Mr. Welton's buttons; they did not provide him with a significant advantage over the other button manufacturers of his day. No, the competitive edge was Merit and his creativity, boldness, and understanding of the role he had to play in his own success. Merit's story reminds one of George Bernard Shaw's great lines, "You see things; and you say, 'Why?' But I dream things that never were; and I say, 'Why not?'"

The selling profession has nothing to do with products or services. It is a profession that deals solely with the interaction between people. Because we in the real estate business basically have the same property available to us through multiple listing, and services offered by all companies are very similar, the personal approach of the salesperson makes all the difference.

If you aspire to great success in real estate sales, you must dare to be different. You will attain great sales success only by establishing an identity and a style that is uniquely your own. People don't do business with companies, but with people. If I'm comfortable with you, I will buy from you. If I'm uncomfortable with you, I will try to avoid buying from you.

Winning is not a matter of luck or good timing. The only way to win big is through good planning and tremendous commitment to execute the plan. Most people who enter the real estate business fail. Statistics tell us that about 60 percent of all people who go into real estate leave in the first six months. Another 20 percent are usually gone at the end of their first twelve months. These legions of hopefuls enter, work for a while, and leave without ever understanding the role they had to play in their own success.

Studies and surveys have been conducted in the

real estate field to determine why buyers and sellers choose one firm over another. An eight-market study of home buyers in the *Newspaper Advertising Bureau* in September 1978 revealed the following breakdown of reasons why buyers chose a certain real estate firm:

1. Knew agent previously   40%
2. Was a past customer of agent   19
3. Agent was recommended   14
4. Newspaper advertising   14
5. Broker respected in area   9
6. Called on for-sale sign   2

This survey and others conducted in recent years all reach the same inescapable conclusion: Customers seek out those salespeople they know or who have been recommended to them. There is a direct relationship between the number of people who perceive you to be a winner and the amount of calls you receive from people seeking you out by name. A good sales strategy and enthusiastic implementation enable you to run your career on purpose rather than by accident.

Where are you in your career? Are you contemplating entering the sales profession for the first time? Have you been in sales for some time with mediocre results? Are you a successful salesperson with an established track record? Whatever your situation may be, the simple truths in this book can help you establish a sales career that will give you all the rewards you ever dreamed were possible.

What do you think it takes to be a sales success? Looks? Personality? Intelligence? Good timing? The right contacts? These are all helpful, but none are essential to realize sales superiority. After 20 years in sales and sales management, I am convinced that the top achievers have two things in common:

1. A tremendous personal commitment to success
2. A plan of action

You may say that sales success depends on many other factors too. It is true that timing, product, territory, competition, and other ingredients play their part. Underlying the importance of all these factors, however, is the dominant role played by commitment and planning.

After reading this book you will be more committed to being a success in sales than you are right now. Once you understand my plan of selling yourself, you will feel that success is more possible than you first imagined. It is my sincere hope that I may have a positive impact on your sales career, thus enabling you to become all you can be.

The most perplexing questions to those in sales management are: Why are a few salespeople superior while most are average or poor? What are the things that a sales manager can do to motivate people? What environment could we create that would lead to sales excellence? How can we spot someone who will succeed versus another who will not succeed? Should I change the commission plan for my people? Should I design a new sales contest that will motivate everyone?

All of these things are tried over and over again on a daily basis all over America. I have come to the conclusion that some people have made a decision to succeed while most people have made no decision at all. The high achievers have resolved to themselves to be the best, regardless of the cost in effort, time, and personal sacrifice. I believe that the question of why one person succeeds while another fails can be answered very simply: One person decides to excel while the other is unwilling to make that decision because of all it entails. Both the superior salesperson and the mediocre salesperson have frustrations, but only the mediocre one has regrets.

So, success is a decision that only you can make for yourself. No amount of coaxing or motivating from some external source will make you a success unless you have decided for yourself that that is what you will be.

A decision of this magnitude will call for your reevaluating your goals and prioritizing those goals. Where does a superior sales career rank on the ladder of those things that are most important to you? It has been said that the goals you choose for yourself should be compatible with each other and should not be in conflict. Do the effort and the rewards of a successful sales career enhance or undermine your major life goals?

It is good for you to get away by yourself from time

to time and look at where your priorities lie. The selling business is not a lark or a hobby that you do while you are waiting around for something else to turn up. It demands great commitment and singlemindedness of purpose if you are going to excel.

Sales success brings with it all the rewards of unlimited income, pride in your accomplishments, and recognition by your peers, as well as the thrill of competition and peace of mind in knowing you can determine your own destiny.

All great salespeople made themselves a pledge that they would prevail and be among the very best in their field. *Have you made that decison? Are you prepared to make that decison now?*

If you are just beginning a sales career, this book can help you formulate a winning strategy that will get you off and running from the start. If you have been in sales for some time with unsatisfactory results, this book can help you rejuvenate your career with a plan that will give you hope and the necessary enthusiasm for your future that you vitally need. If you are doing very well in the sales field, this book can give you ideas that will help you capitalize on your past successes and propel your sales career even faster down the path of success.

This book has been written with one goal in mind: to enable you to devise a strategy that will assure you of superior sales achievement in your chosen profession. Its basic premise is that you must sell yourself first, and then people will buy the goods or services that you offer. Although this may sound obvious or trite, most salespeople fail miserably in their chosen field because they never succeed in establishing a following of potential buyers who seek them out.

The format of this book is rather unusual. Most written works are designed to entertain or to inform. My purpose throughout is to enter into a dialogue with you, the reader. This will be accomplished in the following manner:

1. Each chapter will give you specific facts about the sales business.
2. You will be asked certain probing questions to see how these facts relate to your situation.
3. Blanks will be provided after each question for you to write in your answer.
4. You should, therefore, read this book with a pencil or pen ready to use, and feel free to write anywhere in the book.

Let's roll up our sleeves and get going. Good luck!

The Selling Success Bridge

2

Sales success is a journey. Like any journey, there are some signposts along the way that tell us how far we have come and what lies ahead. In this chapter we discover that a properly designed sales strategy gives us a bridge to avoid falling into the river of failure. The drawing on page 10 tells us in a graphic manner that there are really no short cuts to success.

There is, however, a direct route or there is a roundabout path to take. The direct route is comprised of three separate and distinct stages. All successful salespeople have traveled along this same route on their journeys to fulfilling their goals and ambitions. If we know what lies ahead and what to expect, we can have fun and enjoy the trip because we are safe in the knowledge that we are on the right road. Like most trips we take, the original part of the journey is the most difficult because we are a long way off from our destination and the end is not in sight.

This is also true as you embark on a sales career. In the beginning there is so much to learn and experience that it is at times overwhelming. This is the prospecting stage because your entire time must be devoted to getting out and prospecting for customers.

Selling Success Curve

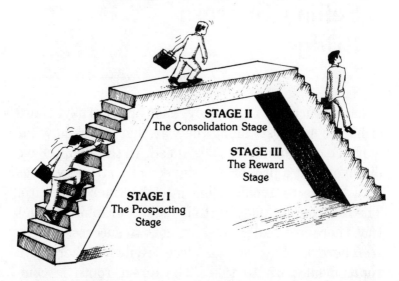

As the old adage dictates, "You have to see the people." Your entire career hinges on how effectively and how consistently you apply yourself to prospecting for new business. Every great salesperson has been good at prospecting for business.

The second stage, called the consolidation stage, is where you really begin to reap the benefits of all your prospecting efforts. The success at this stage depends on how well you have promoted yourself so that potential customers seek you out by name.

Finally, the goal of financial success is at hand as you enter the reward stage. Few people reach this stage. Now your career is in full swing. Past customers are coming back to list their homes with you. New customers are being referred to you because of your successful reputation, and the momentum just continues to build and build. How sweet it is!

Let's examine each of these stages in some depth.

STAGE I: THE PROSPECTING STAGE

This is, beyond a doubt, the most difficult stage of every sales career. As the drawing depicts, it is all uphill. It is up to you alone to begin to build sales. Very few people know you are now in the sales business. You are a virtual unknown competing against proven pros who have been at it a long time.

One of the most trying facts is that there are usually few immediate results for your efforts. You can spend days of relentless effort with very little to show for it. For many people, this is too much to handle and they drop out of sales without ever having enjoyed the sweet taste of success.

Some begin to have anxieties creep into their thinking. Is this the right field for me? Can I hang on long enough to make it go? How far away is success? If you sell big-ticket items, the anxieties are even larger and more frequent. A good real estate salesperson makes three or four sales a month. A new person may not get a signed deal for weeks despite daily effort.

As the name implies, the Prospecting Stage must be composed of a constant effort of getting out to meet people who can give you business. You must find the prospects on your own. Because you have had no past sales, there are no satisfied customers to direct potential buyers your way. In fact, 100 percent of your income will be derived from your present efforts. If you don't get up in the morning and get out there, nothing will happen.

For these reasons, the greatest number of failures occurs in this first stage of a selling career. The people who fail here leave the sales profession, never to return. The tragedy of it is that they never found out what it was really all about. They entered sales not understanding what was essential for winning, and they fought and lost without understanding what was necessary for winning. They usually sum it up by saying sales was not for them. Sales is for anyone who has a good plan and the enthusiasm to carry it out.

Before going on to the next stage, remember one thing: No salesperson is ever done with the chore of prospecting. Sales success is built on repeat customers and *new clients*.

STAGE II: THE CONSOLIDATION STAGE

You will know you have entered this stage when people seek you out by name to do business with you. They have done business with you before, or they know a happy customer of yours, or they have responded to the campaign you have launched for yourself. Stage II marks that portion of your career where you begin making money from your past efforts. You are becoming better known; you have happy customers; referrals are coming your way; your sales success is beginning to pick up momentum. Perhaps 30 percent of your income is the result of your past efforts, and 70 percent is from your continuing prospecting and calling on new potential customers.

Another encouraging fact is that you are beginning to see more frequent results of your work. This, of course, spurs you on to do more because you can feel an increase in confidence that you will make it.

A group of people is beginning to take shape that also believes that you are for real. This group—customers, friends, business associates, acquaintances— will send you leads from time to time so that you are no longer working alone but have the help of more and more people.

Another important difference between this stage and the Prospecting Stage is that your financial situation is looking better. This makes your family a lot happier and more inclined to give you additional encouragement. In direct sales, the only real report card that matters is the size of your pay checks.

Along with an increase in your income comes more enthusiasm for what you're doing. This spills over into everything you do and can increase your effectiveness with potential customers. They will respond to your enthusiasm with a greater inclination to buy. The saying that we are "a drop of intellect in a sea of emotion" is proven over and over in the selling business. The greater the degree of emotion displayed by the salesperson the greater the emotional involvement of the client and the greater the number of sales.

The majority of people who stay in the same sales field for a long time remain in this second stage. They usually remain here for two reasons:

1. They are content with their income level. They have no desire to expend extra effort to make more dollars. They have reached a comfort zone within which they are reasonably satisfied.
2. They are not happy about their income, but it is enough to live on. Although constantly frustrated and not reaching the potential they have hoped for, big success evades them. Sales mediocrity can be the result of many factors. Some of these include no real commitment to excel, no financial pressure to earn more, no encouragement at home, and no personal strategy to beat the competition, as well as a rationalization that they have come far enough, poor self-discipline, and poor time management.

A number of people also drop out of sales after reaching this stage. For them, the income is inadequate, and they either don't believe they can make the additional dollars they need, or they really don't want to pay the price in time and energy to get there.

STAGE III: THE REWARD STAGE

Only 20 percent of all the people entering the sales profession reach this point. This is the real fun part of a sales career. These people are responsible for 80 percent of all the sales written each year.

The unique features of this stage are that 70 percent of your income is the result of all your *past efforts* while only 30 percent comes from continued prospecting for new customers. As the success curve indicates, this stage is like a snowball rolling downhill gaining in speed and size. The momentum of your career has hit full stride. You have many happy customers who refer you to others. The confidence gained from sales success makes you a devastating competitor. Your time is more wisely spent than at any other time because you are continually in the presence of old customers and prospective new ones. Many times, your reputation assures you of the sale before you ever have to make the sales presentation.

Although you are still in a commission business, your annual income is virtually assured at a certain base level because of the growing number of potential customers who seek you out. The group of people who believe you are the best has grown to a number large enough to help you sustain this income. *This huge following and the help they give you is the single reason why people at this stage earn large incomes year after year.*

Needless to say, no one fails at this stage. As long as the salespeople in this stage continue to exert the same characteristics that got them here, their future success and financial security will be guaranteed.

In summary, the only factor that can propel you from one stage to the next is the recognition you have attained in your particular business and the resultant number of people in your following who are there to help your sales volume continue to grow.

People Like a Winner

3

We have now established the fact that highly successful salespeople make their living with the help of many other people. These people are usually motivated by one fact: They believe you are good at what you do.

Why would someone want to help you? Why would people refer you to their friends? Why would anyone want to seek you out to buy from you? They feel they are doing themselves and their friends a favor by referring them to a winner.

We are all attracted to a winner. We like to be around winners. It makes us feel more successful when we are in the company of successful people.

The quickest way to get to the reward stage of your selling career is to impress as many people as possible, in the shortest time, with your ability to do what you do well.

THE BENEFIT OF REFERRALS

Everyone who is at all familiar with the sales field is aware of the benefit of receiving referrals from satisfied customers. There are numerous referral techniques that are taught to aspiring salespeople. We are taught at the consummation of a sale to ask for names of friends or business associates of your new customer. We are taught to keep in touch with past customers who may refer us to someone else or give us repeat business themselves. The shortcoming of most tried-and-true referral techniques is that they don't produce large enough results soon enough to keep a new salesperson going financially and emotionally.

OBSCURITY VS. RECOGNITION

When we think of having a following of people who believe in us, we think of the winners in sports and show business. If you are good at what you do in either of these fields, you will be able to attract a large following, or fan club. This is all possible for one reason: Athletes and actors ply their trade before hundreds and thousands of people at one time. If George Brett were to hit a home run this afternoon, 300,000 people would immediately be aware of it. Those 300,000 would tell another 300,000 and, after repeated successes before thousands of people, George Brett would be firmly entrenched in the minds of many people as one of the greatest sluggers of all time.

On the other hand, if I were to sell a $200,000 home this afternoon, who knows about it? Probably the buyer, the seller, and a few neighbors and friends. I would be every bit as successful in my chosen profession as George is in his. However, I did not have 300,000 people looking on. I sold that home in an atmosphere of almost total obscurity. If we are to begin to develop a following, we must lift our successes out of the darkness of obscurity into the bright sunlight of recognition. Every good salesperson finds a way to do just that.

It is not enough to be good at what you do. Many of your competitors are also very good. If you and I are competitors with equal talents and work habits, it would appear that we would probably enjoy equal success. Not true. The difference in our incomes will be measured by the number of people who know me as a winner versus the number who know you as a winner. If I have 1,500 people who are aware of my success and you have 800, I am assured of larger earning potential because I will have almost twice as many people helping me.

Salespeople all over the world are succeeding, but their careers are growing at a snail's pace because they are doing it in a self-imposed environment of obscurity. The point is this: Don't go through all the blood, sweat, and tears to get a successful sale without getting all the recognition you can. Every past sale properly promoted can lead to many more sales in the future. Build on each success to yield new ones. Don't let them die unnoticed.

ARE WINNERS BORN OR MADE?

We have all heard that tired cliché, he is a "born salesman." Another says that salesmen are born not made. Either you have it or you don't. If true, we are all born to success or failure. Our careers are subject to some all-encompassing law of predestination. Should you believe these axioms? No.

Salespeople are made, not born. Yes, some enter the sales field with more raw talent than others. But those with the talent fail as often as everybody else. All the education, good looks, or communication skills that one may possess do not determine success in sales. I really cannot tell by any interviewing techniques now available how badly a person *wants* to succeed. You'll notice that I said wants to succeed not needs to succeed. Many people need to be successful in order to feed their family, but they still fail. The person who really *wants* to will succeed.

Anyone can be made into a top salesperson. The only person who will be a big winner in the selling field, however, is the salesperson who is *self-made*. Yes, salespeople can be made if they are not born natural salespersons. But they can only be self-made. That inner drive that makes top people go can only come from within themselves.

HOW DO THE TOP WINNERS CREATE THE INNER DRIVE?

Salespeople are self-made with two necessary ingredients: a *clear vision* of themselves as a success and the *self-commitment* to go for it. Do you see yourself as becoming a big winner in your chosen field of sales? Every person who has reached the top in sales believed it was possible all along. They always had the vision of themselves at the top of their sales organization. The vision was so attractive and desirable to them that it sustained them through the tough times that every salesperson endures. Not only did it sustain them, it became an unfulfilled promise that drove them until it became a fulfilled promise. It was the realization of this vision that got them to the top and the thrill of it that kept them there. The money they made along the way was only the report card but not the real reward.

It is not enough to have a vision of yourself as a success. A daydreamer can do that much. The second necessary ingredient of a self-made salesperson is the self-commitment to make that vision a reality. Many of us can probably see ourselves as the top dog in our company. But how many of us are prepared to exert the necessary energies to reach the top?

This topic of self-commitment is the bottom line of every sales career. Without the vision of success, there would be no need for a commitment to see that vision come true. But without the commitment, the vision is a dream and nothing more. The kind of self-commitment needed to make it to the top is the result of *you* sitting down with *you* to establish what *you* want for yourself. How does this vision of sales success rank with the other priorities of your life? Is it really worth the effort and personal dedication necessary to see it through? How much are you committed to it? Is your family committed to it?

If you have never given too much thought to the vision of yourself in sales and considered the necessary commitment to fulfilling that vision, do so now.

The commitment necessary to excel in sales is the same quality you will need to make effective use of the ideas we will explore together in later chapters.

A smart plan, designed to sell you as a winner in the sales field, combined with your commitment to realizing your vision of yourself, will make you unstoppable.

How
Salable
Are You?

4

Is real estate the right field for you? Did you enter the real estate business to become wealthy? The late J. Paul Getty, one of the world's richest men, said that you need three ingredients to attain great wealth:

1. You must be in business for yourself.
2. You must offer a product or service people want.
3. You must earn through the efforts of other people.

Well, as a real estate salesperson, you are certainly in business for yourself. You and you alone will determine how successful you will be. So the real estate business satisfies the first criterion for financial success.

The real estate sales field addresses itself to one of the four basic needs of all people, which are food, clothing, shelter, and safety. Because you provide one of the four basic needs, there will always be demand for your services.

The third criterion for wealth, income through the efforts of others, is usually overlooked by the average real estate salesperson. This book has been written to address the topic of building a following of people who use their own efforts to refer you to potential customers, to sing your praises as a truly competent and successful person, and to seek you out when they have real estate needs of their own.

Of course, you only sell one item in the real estate business—yourself. In order to maximize your salability, let us look at a number of key factors.

YOUR COMPETITION

Who are your competitors? In order to answer this question, you have to decide in what area you will be working to earn the majority of your income. If you are going to stay within a five-mile radius of your office, then you should look at the specific residential areas that you know are very active in terms of sales. Drive through the streets and write down the names on the other real estate for-sale signs. You should also consult your multiple listing book to see if one or two real estate people dominate most of the sales in the area. If no one seems to be dominant, you have a good opportunity to take the area over. If one or two people do get the majority of the business, can they be beaten?

When I looked at the area I wanted to work in, I discovered that one woman was quite effective and had been working in the area for 27 years. The area had 1,300 homes with about eight sales every month. She accounted for two or three sales a month. I decided that I could take the business away from her because she was not working as hard as she had in the early years, and she did not have an effective method of keeping her name and face before the homeowners on a regular basis. I designed a newsletter that included my photo and helpful hints for the homeowners. This newsletter was mailed to each owner every month. After eight months, I was selling 40 percent of all the homes sold. This grew to 70 percent after 12 months. So, if you find a strong competitor, analyze his or her tactics for promoting themselves to the neighborhood. You may be able to unseat them with a superior promotion plan.

Take out a sheet of paper and write down why a homeowner should list with your competitor, and then make a list of reasons why someone should list with you. If the competitor is with a small firm and yours is larger, point out the peace of mind in dealing with a financially secure, full-service company. If your company is small and the competitor is larger, stress the advantage of the personal service and caring attitude of a smaller company. List some of the personal services you provide each of your sellers such as:

1. An open house twice each month.
2. A call after each showing to keep them informed.
3. A weekly status call to let them know everything you are doing and what the current market activity is.
4. A copy of every advertisement on the house mailed to them.
5. A monthly pricing and marketing review.

Think about what you offer versus what your competitor offers. You must already have or you must create an edge that will persuade homeowners to choose you instead of your competitor.

Three years after I started my newsletter, a new real estate company opened across the street from me with the purpose of taking away the business that I had built up and nourished with a lot of hard work. Its proprietor was a very honest and respectable man. He even had the courtesy to come across the street on the day he opened and announce to me that he was going to drive me out of this hot area that I now dominated. He worked for two and a half years to beat me. At one time, he had 10 salespeople on his staff. But I still got the majority of the listings due primarily to my newsletter and my personal involvement in the subdivision affairs. I joined the swim club, dance club, and recreation commission. I lived there and all six of my children went to school and played on Little League teams with the children of other homeowners. The other broker lived about five miles away and was not involved in the community.

YOUR PRESENTATION

Do you have a good listing presentation? Is it your own or someone else's? Do you feel comfortable with it? Do you use visual aids?

In 1977 a nationwide study was conducted to determine the role of our five senses in the learning process.

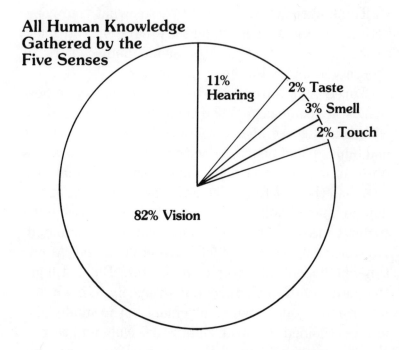

All Human Knowledge
Gathered by the
Five Senses

11%
Hearing

2% Taste

3% Smell

2% Touch

82% Vision

(See the diagram above.) This proves that the sense of sight accounts for 82 percent of all the knowledge absorbed and retained by the human mind. The message is clear. Don't just tell. *Show* and tell. Remember, sell the benefits to the customer, not just the facts about you and your service.

How much of your presentation is dedicated to selling the benefits of choosing you as an individual? Inject your own personality into your presentation. Let the prospect get to know you as a person. People do business with people they like. Allow a relationship to develop between you and your prospect so that he or she is talking to a friend by the time your presentation is concluded. It is hard to say no to a friend.

I had a picture of my family in my visual presentation. I would ask them about their family. We always had something in common. I would include testimonial letters from satisfied customers. I would also have photos of other homes that I had successfully sold in the immediate neighborhood. A picture is still worth a thousand words.

Include your prospects in the presentation. Ask them questions as you go along so you can constantly monitor how they are reacting to what you are saying.

Is your presentation the right length? It is too short if you have not made your case in a simple and convincing manner. It is too long if you went past the point where the prospect is ready to sign up with you. Remember, your primary objective is not to finish the presentation. It is to get the order. Your prospect may be ready to sign up with you without a presentation because you may have come highly recommended by a trusted friend. If so, forget the presentation. Get the signature!

HONESTY AND INTEGRITY

No salesperson of any stature built a career on the "fast buck" kind of mentality. As in any other area of life, bad news always spreads faster than good news. Dishonesty and deception can sometimes facilitate a quick sale, but they will just as quickly cause the early demise of a sales career. In the final analysis, your long-run career potential will be held hostage by the way you have treated your customers along the way. When selling yourself, your personal reputation is your most treasured possession.

In my first year of selling I met a salesman who had been in the business a long time. We got to talking about the value of honesty and integrity in real estate sales and he told me of a most interesting thing that had happened to him. He was showing homes to a transferee and his wife one day when the customers found a home they were particularly thinking of buying. The asking price on the house was $55,000. The transferee asked him at what price he could purchase this home. The salesman replied that he could buy it for $55,000. The transferee said he knew he could pay the full price but how much less would the seller accept? The salesman replied that he had no knowledge that the seller would accept any less but that he would present an offer of the transferee's choosing and see what the seller's reply would be. Eventually they negotiated a price acceptable to both buyer and seller. Four years later, the salesperson received a phone call from that transferee who now wanted to sell the home that he had purchased four years earlier. He told the salesman that he admired the way he had represented the seller by not suggesting a price less than the official asking price, and he wanted the same kind of representation now that he was on the selling end of the transaction.

SELF-DISCIPLINE

Another significant attribute of the top salespeople in any sales field is self-discipline. The tremendous freedom available to a salesperson can be the undoing of many who do not have the self-discipline to handle their time wisely. The salesperson's time is best spent in the immediate presence of someone who is a potential customer. Top producers put a rigid code of daily discipline into their workday so that they are in the best possible place to obtain orders. In my experience, strong self-discipline is necessary in four important areas:

1. **Time management.** Salespeople are probably the greatest time wasters of anyone in the business world. They have so much free time, and they don't use it wisely. There have been many books written about this subject, and I'm sure many more will follow. Suffice it to say that improper use of that precious commodity, time, will be and has been the downfall of many sales aspirants. The simplest tool I ever saw for good time management is a daily planner that can be purchased at any office-supply store. Of course, time management is not as easy as carrying a book to record appointments. Self-discipline is the deciding factor between a day well spent and a day wasted. How many hours a day do you spend in the presence of a potential customer?

2. **Making the cold call.** Have you mastered the art of making the cold call? Most successful sales people at some time in their careers had to make cold calls or "beat the bushes" to drum up business. In search of business, have you ever initiated an in-person cold call on a total stranger? It takes courage to do it once. It takes self-discipline to do it continually.

3. **Follow through on the details.** Necessary in any sales career is the proper handling of details. Although most super salespeople are not "detail oriented," processing of orders, servicing the customer, closing the sale, and periodic follow-up require self-discipline. Many salespeople have successfully gotten the order only to lose the sale because of inadequate follow-through. The potential customer who looked forward to buying your product or service now is telling others not to buy from you. This is a common occurrence in the sales business. Most sales forces have some kind of organization behind them to handle many of the details. This may be true in your case. But never forget, no one is as interested in your customer's well-being as you. You are ultimately responsible for his or her happiness and you will be held accountable for how the customer is treated by your firm.

4. **Overcoming negative influences.** A salesperson has to believe that success is possible. A true salesperson is a hopeless optimist. Around you, however, there are always constant negative influ-

ences. It could be the general economy or the current economic health of your particular industry. The two groups that have the greatest influence on you are your family and your fellow sales associates.

Let's talk about the influence of your family. If your family is skeptical about your career in sales or downright negative about your chance of success, the need for commitment and self-discipline is *total*. The need for communication between you and your family is particularly important at the outset of your sales career. They should be informed about what you will be facing both from the viewpoint of challenge and of potential success. Your family can help increase your success by being supportive, flexible about accepting your hours, helpful with your wardrobe, and reasonable about financial demands until you have hit your stride.

Every sales office has its prophets of doom and gloom. The most dangerous place in every office is around the coffee pot where the losers in the office wax eloquently about the sheer impossibility of it all. They like to get hold of the new rookies and fill them full of doubts so that they can further justify their own mediocrity. The negative influences in sales offices have claimed many victims over the years. These time wasters and positive-attitude killers must be avoided always. This will take a tough mental attitude and a strict adherence to your daily game plan.

PHYSICAL QUALITIES

What is the physical image that you present to a would-be customer? Are you and your clothing clean and well groomed? You must look successful before anyone will think that you are. How about posture? Someone who is erect obviously has self-pride, while the stooped look denotes a lack of self-confidence.

Your handshake tells a lot about you. A firm handshake is important to a salesperson. Your briefcase and pen, although seemingly unimportant, can add or subtract from the winning image that you want to convey. Last, the car you drive to an appointment can leave an impression. You should choose the kind of car you drive as it relates to the type of customers you have in your industry. You must decide whether the conservative or flamboyant look will do you the most good in the eye of your potential client. Regardless of the style, it should be clean and well maintained.

HOW DO YOU COMPARE?

One of the rules of good public speaking is that no one should address an audience unless that person has the right to be on the podium. This right is earned only by those people who know their subject well and are prepared to deliver it to their listeners. The same is true of the salesperson. You have not earned the right to sell me your product or service until you understand how it will benefit me and why I should buy from you to the exclusion of all others.

The Harvard Business Review, in June 1982, carried an article that said the necessary ingredient in everyone's work is a phrase called "clarity of task." The point being made was that we can accomplish much more in our daily work life if our objective is clear and easy to understand. So, like the public speaker, you must be prepared for your vocation of selling. The clear task is not to proceed into the next chapter until you have taken a good look at yourself and assessed how you compare in the areas of your product or service, your competition, your presentation, your honesty and integrity, your self-discipline, and your physical qualities.

After a careful review, target in on those areas that need further improvement. Make a prioritized list of the areas that you will work on and a deadline by which each one will be accomplished. The chart on the following page may be helpful for this purpose.

AREAS FOR IMPROVEMENT

Satisfactory (S) Unsatisfactory (U)	Area Of Improvement
	Product Knowledge — Do You Know Home Values?
	Competitive Knowledge — How Do You Handle the Competition?
	Point of Sale Presentation — Do You Have a Visual Presentation?
	Self Discipline — Time Management — What Is Your Daily Schedule?
	Self Discipline — Making Cold Calls — How Many a Week?
	Self Discipline — Follow Through — Do You Keep in Touch?
	Self Discipline — Overcoming Negative Influences — Do You Stick with Your Plan?
	Honesty and Integrity — How About It?
	Physical Qualities — Clothing — Get Another Opinion
	Physical Qualities — Grooming — Regularly?
	Physical Qualities — Posture
	Physical Qualities — Automobile — Is It Appropriate for Your Kind of Customer?
	Physical Qualities — Handshake

Where Are You in the Fleet?

5

Now that we have looked at you and your ability, let's look around us in the real estate sales field. The real estate brokerage business is composed of some of the following statistics (as of December 1984), gathered by the economics and research division of the National Association of Realtors:

Number of existing single-family home sales
    annually   3,000,000
Number of new single-family home sales
    annually   641,000
Approximate number of firms   120,000
Approximate number of salespeople   1,200,000
Median income of full-time sales
    associates $18,000
Median income of part-time sales
    associates $6,400
Male sales associates   42.6%
Female sales associates   57.4%
Average age of sales associates   44 years
Average years of real estate sales
    experience   5 years
Bachelor's degree or better   36.6%

Average hours worked per week	42 hours
Residential brokerage specialty	81.6%
Commercial brokerage specialty	3.9%
Real estate sales main source of income	80%
Average sale price per transaction	$72,600

What do these statistics tell us about the competitive climate of real estate sales?

Conclusion 1. There is an average sales price of $72,600 per transaction. If the average fee charged to the sellers is 6 percent of the sales price and if you receive roughly 50 percent of the commission paid to your broker, you would be paid approximately $1,500 per sale.

Conclusion 2. Transactions totalling 3,641,000 a year amount to an industry with total commissions to sales associates of $5,461,500,000.

Conclusion 3. If this $5,461,500,000 were divided equally among all 1,200,000 salespeople nationally, it would mean an annual income for each sales associate of $4,551. Obviously, the income is not divided equally. The field is comprised of the haves and the have-nots. This statistic does, however, point up the necessity to rise above the mediocre averages in order to earn a respectable income.

Conclusion 4. The United States has an approximate population of 250 million people. With 1.2 million licensed real estate sales associates, one out of every 208 men, women, and children has a real estate license. Granted, they are not dispersed equally across the country. Nevertheless, the point still remains that it will take some ingenuity and commitment in order to get more than your share of business.

Conclusion 5. If you think you will earn a lot of money selling real estate on a part-time basis, forget it. The statistics show that the average income of people who work part time is $6,400.

Conclusion 6. Here is an interesting fact. The average salesperson you will be up against has been in the real estate business only five years or less. Some of these people have had one year of experience five times. They are really not any more of a threat in their fifth year than they were in their first year.

A few, meanwhile, have been putting out the effort and developing their skills. These people are probably earning five times as much as the first group of people who are waiting for their luck to change.

Conclusion 7. The average full-time hours worked per week are 42 hours. This business does demand a lot of your time. The top-producing salespeople mentioned later in this book spend in the 50- to 70-hour range each week. The best way I know to lessen the number of hours is to concentrate on getting listings instead of showing houses. Three hours of preparation and actual presentation are needed to secure listings. With buyers, you must be ready when they are. Buyers need to be taken to many homes in order to learn about the market and find the home they want to buy. It could take from five to twenty hours to find the right home and negotiate the sale.

Conclusion 8. The profile of your average competitor is as follows:

1. Female
2. Age 44 years
3. Been in the business less than 5 years
4. Main livelihood is real estate sales
5. Works at least 42 hours a week
6. Basically specializing in residental sales
7. Does not have a college degree

As we have learned from these statistics, this business is very, very competitive. For the remainder of this chapter, let's look at the competitive forces at work and how they affect us.

An article in the June 1982 issue of *Yachting* magazine deals with the role that mental attitude plays in a sailboat race. Unlike most theories dealing with sail design, crew experience, hull shape, and weather conditions, this article maintained that the mental attitude of the boat's skipper was the deciding factor between victory and defeat.

Most sailors in any metropolitan area find themselves competing against the same people every weekend. After a while, each skipper begins unknowingly to visualize where he or she will finish as the boats cross the finish line. The skipper who always wins has a mental picture of winning before the race starts. Other boat captains picture themselves finishing somewhere down the line but not in first place. The sailor who often finishes last would be delighted to finish second to last for a change.

The article referred to this phenomenon as the "hierarchy of the fleet." It is an unconscious admission by the racers that each participant has self-imposed limitations that will prevent him or her from winning. The skipper who always wins believes he or she will continue to win while the others believe that they will not win but that they will finish better than they have before.

For some time my family lived on a lake on which no motorized craft were allowed. Most of the homeowners on the lake had an interest in sailing. In fact, every Sunday during the summer there was a sailing race at 11:00 A.M. Each boat allowed on the lake was exactly the same design and specifications as every other boat. Each boat had a crew of two. One of the boats had a red-and-white striped sail while all the others were plain white. Week after week the red-and-white striped sail finished first. I became accustomed to it as I watched from the shore. I guess the racers became accustomed to it also. My neighbor directly across the lake always finished last. The boats between first and last place would switch around a little from week to week, but they never finished first or last. I guess their skippers had established an unconscious hierarchy in their minds of how they would perform.

A salesperson is exactly like one of those skippers in the race for success. All of us draw limits in our minds. A few of us picture ourselves winning, while most see a finish somewhere down in the pack. This picture we have of ourselves can be an all-consuming one. It can dictate how we approach our whole life. Those who picture themselves winning live with gusto and a sense of urgency. They have to achieve great things in order to live up to the image they have of themselves, while others put in an average effort to support the average results they expect.

YOUR SALES STAFF

Every sales staff has its own personality. Every branch office of every company has unique individuals who relate to one another in different ways. There is also, however, a certain sameness to every sales staff. There is usually one sales leader, a couple of other good producers, a larger number of average sales people, and some low producers. Everyone on the sales staff understands the situation and where he or she is in relationship to the others around. In addition to knowing where they are, most people who have been a member of the staff also accept their position as some kind of inevitable happening.

Most new salespeople start out their careers with a high degree of optimism and a feeling that anything is possible. After spending time in the sales business and after comparing themselves with the other salespeople in their office, they begin unconsciously to position themselves somewhere in the pack. After more time in the presence of the same people, they become more resigned to their positions in relation to everyone else. Eventually the pattern is set in their minds, and they spend the rest of their sales careers living up to or living down to their self-established images. The hierarchy that is established is great if you are the top banana. It's self-defeating if you are at the bottom of the totem pole. For this reason the positions don't change very often. The top person has to continue to strive because he or she has enjoyed the recognition of being the best. To be anything other than the top person would be devastating to the self-image that has been reinforced through adulation of the whole peer group.

The pressure that keeps the top person running hard is the same pressure that prevents the low person from striving to move up. After repeated reminders that he or she is the lowest, this person no longer believes that success is possible. So, rather than giving the top person a good contest, he or she gives up entirely and loses by forfeiture.

This pressure of the hierarchy within your office has a large and constant impact on your mental attitude. If you are near the top, you are positively motivated by your standing within the group. If you are in the middle of the pack, you may be rather comfortable and not too motivated by your standing other than to maintain your position. If you are near the bottom, you are continually reminded that you're not doing as well as those around you. This could serve as a positive inducement to do better if you have a strong positive self-image. For most people near the bottom, it will tend to reinforce a poor self-image and low achievement.

YOUR INDUSTRY

In addition to the hierarchy in your office, a larger one exists within your industry between competing firms. As a data processing salesman for IBM 20 years ago, I always felt that my product, service, and company reputation were the best in the computer industry. How do you feel your company rates in your industry? What position does it have in relation to those you must compete with?

The hierarchy between companies as you perceive it can also greatly affect your effectiveness in a sales confrontation with a competitor. When you find out you are competing for a specific listing, you probably react differently against one company than against another. You may get beaten rather regularly by one particular firm because of price, quality, service, or the selling skills of its sales force. After repeated losses to this company, you will begin to put them ahead of you as an unbeatable foe. You may even find yourself unconsciously giving up in a head-to-head battle with them.

When competing against companies that are not as awesome in your mind, you probably approach the prospective customer with more confidence and a greater sense of self-assurance. Because you have established this unconscious hierarchy in your mind, you automatically react differently.

ARE THEY BETTER THAN YOU?

The question that must finally be asked of the sailors who compete every Sunday is: "Is the skipper of the boat with the red-striped sail better than all the rest and therefore unbeatable?" Is the top person in your office better than you and unbeatable? Is the competitor who beats you regularly better than you and unbeatable? The answer to all three questions is a resounding NO! No one is better than anyone else. The difference is that they are doing a better job than you at the present time. They can be beaten! By you!

The Salesperson and the Politician

6

Vic Caputo is probably not a familiar name to you. After enjoying a broadcasting career that spanned 23 years on Detroit radio and television stations, however, he was easily recognized by thousands of Detroiters. In 1980 Vic left his career in broadcasting to run for the office of United States Congressman from the 14th district in suburban Detroit. His opponent was a lesser known person by the name of Dennis Hertel who was then a state representative.

Because of his tremendous media recognition, it would be fair to say that Vic Caputo began the campaign with an advantage over his challenger. Vic did all the normal things that political aspirants usually do. He gave speeches, visited various groups, sent out mailings, urged people to vote on election day, and other common campaigning tactics.

But Dennis Hertel did something different and daring. He personally went to the door of 6,000 potential voters asking for their vote on election day. Rather than relying on the conventional approaches, he decided to go at the voters one at a time in their own homes. The weather can get pretty rough during the months of September, October, and November in Michigan, but Dennis was not deterred from his door-to-door campaign. His strategy was time consuming and physically exhausting.

How would you feel about a political candidate who came to your door to ask for your vote? You might reach the following conclusions:

1. The candidate put a high value on the importance of your vote.
2. The candidate was a hard worker.
3. The candidate really wanted this political office.
4. The candidate was prepared to try new ideas.
5. The candidate was a goal-oriented and self-confident person.
6. Any candidate who would make that kind of effort deserved your vote.

Dennis Hertel did the impossible. He beat his well-known opponent with his spectacular door-to-door campaign. He won the election because he understood the two things one must do to win:

1. Do something your competitor is not willing to do.
2. Provide people an additional reason to choose you.

Your challenge in building your own real estate career is identical to that of Dennis Hertel. When you enter the business, you are an unknown competing against many well-known, solidly entrenched sales professionals. You have to hit the ground running with a strategy that will propel your personal visibility and success story to as many potential customers as soon as possible before you exhaust your financial and emotional resources. You don't have unlimited time to begin earning a decent income just as Dennis didn't have unlimited time before election day. You must earn a certain sum of money within a restricted time period or you will not attain the necessary momentum needed to carry you to high earnings from real estate sales.

Later in this book we will explore the personal success stories of other salespeople who designed and implemented their own unique campaigns for sales supremacy.

Before we do that, however, let us examine the parallels between the life of a salesperson and that of a politician.

UNKNOWN VS. INCUMBENT

The Politician Every new aspirant to political office has to take on the more experienced and better known current officeholder.

The Salesperson As a new salesperson, you are suddenly thrust into the marketplace to compete against experienced salespeople, some of whom are old pros who are well entrenched. You are virtually unknown and unproven in this particular field.

NEED TO IDENTIFY A CONSTITUENCY

The Politician Someone running for public office must do some homework to decide where his or her votes will come from. If you are running for

the job of mayor of your city, you aren't concerned about anyone other than those residents of the city who are registered to vote.

The Salesperson Not everyone is a potential buyer for your product or service. You must, therefore, identify who your potential customers are and where they are located.

A CAMPAIGN IS NECESSARY

The Politician When running for office, planning begins months ahead of election day. Some of the things to be considered are the number and whereabouts of potential voters, the ideas that will appeal to them, the traits one possesses that make one a different candidate, the approach to be used in promoting oneself in person and through the use of the mass media and the print media. A master plan or campaign is then developed for implementation.

The Salesperson   In order to beat your competition regularly, you must consider all the same points listed for the politician and design a plan that will build your career on purpose rather than by accident.

NAME RECOGNITION IS A MUST

The Politician   The goal of every politician is to make his or her name a household word. Large numbers of people must know who the politician is and what he or she does.

The Salesperson   In order to generate a large sales volume, many people must be able to equate your name with what you do for a living. When hearing your name, they must also identify you as being very good at what you do.

Are you now convinced that the two careers are indeed very similar? If so, let's learn and use some of the techniques that a politician uses. Both politicians and sales people must face an incumbent, identify a constituency, design a campaign, and build a name for themselves. The first thing every aspiring political candidate must do is identify who and where the potential voters are. Likewise, you must begin by finding out who and where your potential buyers are.

Who Is Your Constituency?

7

A constituency is a group of supporters. The politician knows that winning an election is possible only through the help of many people. So, before any other plans are made, the candidate must identify who the potential members of his or her constituency are. They must be convinced that the candidate is worthy of their support both in terms of time and effort. Once they are won over, their loyalty serves as the backbone that assures the steady progress of the politician's career. This is why an incumbent who has had many years to expand the size of his or her constituency is so hard to beat.

You also need a group of supporters who remain loyal to you over the years. Most salespeople begin each day as if it were their first day in the selling business. The big earners have learned the value of a strong constituency, and they begin each day with many helpers who are prepared to refer someone to them or to buy from them themselves. You must identify people who will buy from you directly or who will refer you to others. The number of people who think you're good determines the sales volume you will write each year.

How do you carve out your fair portion of the

49

potential buyers? *The easiest approach is to choose those people with whom you share something in common. People like to do business with people they like. They are more comfortable dealing with someone they can relate to.* Members of your potential following may belong to one of the following groups.

FAMILY

Friends and acquaintances of your family are probably the strongest constituency you will have. Strong personal and emotional bonds built up over the years cannot be matched by most other relationships. People in this group need only be acquainted with one member of your family in order for their loyalty and patronage to be transferred to you and to what you are selling. They may know your spouse, children, parents, in-laws, grandchildren, grandparents, nieces, nephews, uncles, aunts, or any other relative. A good group to contact with ties to your child would be the school's parent-teacher organization. Your father may belong to a retirement group or lodge. Fellow employees who work at your spouse's place of business should be considered. What groups could be contacted through some affiliation of a member of your family?

ETHNIC GROUP

Second in order of potential loyalty are the other members of your ethnic group. If many people in your ethnic group do not speak English well, they will be strongly attracted to someone who can relate to them in their native tongue. A roster of those who belong to any ethnic social organizations could become an ideal prospect list for you. Many members of ethnic groups live in close proximity to each other. Some ethnic groups publish newspapers and/or newsletters that could provide ideal advertising exposure for you. Do you have an ethnic affiliation?

RELIGIOUS AFFILIATION

A strong common bond between you and others is a mutual religious affiliation. Members of your particular congregation are an excellent source for participation in your constituency. Membership on certain committees within your religious institution can also bring you in contact with people in a personal way. When membership in a particular religious group also encompasses a certain ethnic affiliation, you have the two unifying factors of religion and ethnic heritage, both of which are strong bonds. Regional or national mailing lists are usually available if you want to extend your constituency beyond the confines of your own congregation. Do you have a religious affiliation?

ALUMNI GROUPS

People who share a common experience always enjoy a special relationship with each other. Your previous elementary, secondary, college, or other schooling history makes you a bona fide member of several bodies of people who have shared a unique experience. Those classmates of yours are making decisions to buy and sell things every day. They are also referring other people to do likewise. Use the special relationship you have with them to make them an important part of your constituency. Mailing lists are usually available from the schools you have attended. Are you a member of an alumni association that can help you?

PREVIOUS FELLOW EMPLOYEES

If you have had previous work experience with an organization, the friends and acquaintances you made while there could be the source of future business. They know you as a person, and you probably shared many common work experiences with them.

A man in Kansas City, Missouri, who recently retired from a large automobile plant where he had worked for 35 years, said he had always been interested in becoming a real estate salesman but he didn't know if he could be a success at his age and with no prior selling experience. He had worked in every department of a plant that employed 5,000 people. All of those 5,000 people have real estate needs occasionally and have friends who do also. His 35 years of making friends in the plant could guarantee him many years as a successful salesman if these valuable contacts were developed properly.

One of the most successful salespeople I ever met was a woman who entered real estate sales after many years as a waitress in a small-town restaurant. Everyone in town knew and liked her as a waitress. They transferred that loyalty to her as a real estate salesperson and she immediately began a meteoric climb up the ladder of sales success to become the top person of an 800-person organization.

Think about your previous work experience. Are there people with previous employers who can help you build your sales career?

SOCIAL/RECREATIONAL GROUPS

Dance clubs, card clubs, gardening, sports, exercise groups all fit into this category. Any group you belong to for the purpose of relaxing and enjoying the companionship of others is a source of potential business. These organizations usually have a mailing list that would be helpful. What groups do you belong to?

PROFESSIONAL GROUPS

Included in this category would be all the professional associations that are identified by the type of members they serve. Doctors have the American Medical Association; attorneys have the American Bar Association; union members have their particular union with a local of which they are a member; war veterans have veteran groups. Almost every field of endeavor has some kind of professional association available to those involved in that type of work. What professional groups do you now or have you in the past belonged to?

PAST CUSTOMERS

Past customers are an excellent source of future business. Having once purchased from your firm, they are believable when recommending your company to someone else. If you have been in the sales business for a while and have compiled your own group of past customers, you have a great opportunity to get good referrals from these people. What program do you have to keep in touch with your past customers?

If you are new in the selling profession and do not have past customers, you still have the opportunity to use this excellent base of referrals. Every company has past customers whose original salesperson is no longer with the company. The chances are that no one is following up with these people on a regular basis. Check with your sales manager to see if such a list can be obtained. Because of your affiliation with the company, that past customer now becomes your past customer.

Before leaving this chapter, let us identify whom you are going to choose as your constituency.

- Which group or groups have you chosen?
- Will the people you have identified give you the best chance of success when compared to any other choices you might have?

- How many people have you selected?
- Have you picked enough people to give you the sales volume you need?
- Have you found a source of information whereby you can identify everyone in your group by name and address?

If you are satisfied with the answers you have given, let us proceed.

Designing Your Campaign

8

In this chapter, we are going to explore all of the most successful campaigns that are working well for top-producing salespeople from coast to coast. Before getting into specific techniques, however, we must first understand two basic programs that we refer to as farming systems.

A farming system is an organized plan of promoting yourself and your credentials to a specifically identified group of people. This plan calls for repeated efforts on your part to render service, make friends, and convince this targeted group that you are a winner in the real estate business.

These two concepts require hard work and a great investment in terms of time, energy, and dollars on your part. They also can enable you to originate, sustain, and build a rewarding career in real estate sales. These two systems are called social and geographic farming.

SOCIAL FARMING

People like to do business with people they know! This is a basic premise of the selling profession. Social farming is the identification and development of a specific group of people without attention to where they live.

In the previous chapter entitled *Who Is Your Constituency?* we listed many types of social-farming targets. Let us take one of these target groups and explore how we can develop it to our advantage. Suppose you belong to a religious group of some kind. There are some fundamental questions to answer when designing the best strategy for you.

Do the majority of members own homes in areas that you can properly service? If you want to spend a lot of time, money, and effort promoting yourself to this group, be certain that you will get listings in areas you are familiar with and that are close enough to ensure that you can give them good service. If the congregants live all over town, you could be listing properties that you may be pricing improperly and servicing poorly. This, of course, could lead to disaster as the word gets around the membership that you don't do a good job with the confidence they place in you. Conversely, if many members own homes in neighborhoods that you know and can handle, your efforts can pay off handsomely.

How many members own homes in your servicing area? Don't forget that the selling business is a numbers game! If 1,000 members own homes in your servicing area, you can justify pursuing a strategy in this religious group. If, however, only 200 people live in your area, forget it. Think big. If you don't think big, big things don't happen.

How will you participate? You could volunteer to become a reader at the religious services. This would put you in front of the membership on a regular basis. Perhaps you could join a committee of the church or synagogue. This would put you in close and regular contact with various members that you may not otherwise know well. Most religious groups have a hierarchy of some sort. Certain people hold some official position in the church or synagogue. These positions are usually visible, and the people who occupy them are well known. A certain amount of campaigning is inherent in getting appointed or elected. This process of campaigning could give you exposure to the entire membership.

What kind of functions does this group have each year? Most groups have annual functions such as a Halloween party, annual family picnic, Christmas dance, or Thanksgiving dinner. You could chair the committee that puts one of these events together. You could provide prizes as a promotional idea. Volunteer to do something at each function. It doesn't have to be a consuming job you take on. Each function gives you an opportunity to meet and interact with new people. Volunteer work of this kind will usually put you in touch with the most active people in the religious group. These are the people who get around a lot and talk to many other members in a year's time. They can do you a lot of good if they feel you are involved as they are and dedicated to the same values. Often people will go out of their way to give business leads because you are one of them.

Does the organization have a periodic publication of some kind? Most religious groups publish a bulletin, newspaper, newsletter, or something similar. Could you purchase an ad in this publication? If so, be sure to include a professional photo in the ad and remind the readers that you are a member of the church or synagogue. Many people will give business to a congregant they have not met before they would give business to an unaffiliated stranger they have also not met. The photo will help those people who have seen you at religious functions but did not know your name. If ads are not available, perhaps you could submit articles or help with the gathering of information for the publication. This could give you a legitimate reason to be in contact with many people and also be aware of everything that is happening.

Does the organization sponsor any youth-related activities? The best way to get through to someone is through their kids. You can make a friend for life by helping someone's child in some way. The parents feel they owe you a debt of gratitude and usually will repay that debt with business if they know you are in the real estate business. Social events for teenagers such as dances or parties provide you an opportunity to be a chaperone. Most houses of worship need people to help with preschoolers while the adults are at the service.

Churches or synagogues often sponsor athletic teams. Perhaps you could play on or attend adult athletic games. You could coach or assist the children's teams. Regular contact with the kids and parents at both practices and games could give you great visibility and will promote a sense of gratitude from the parents.

Can you obtain a mailing list of the entire membership? This can be an invaluable tool for you if one is available. You could on a regular basis send your fellow members greeting cards, letters, just-listed and just-sold cards, newsletters, and any other promotional items that you deem appropriate. Maybe you might volunteer to pay for and compile the mailing pieces to notify the membership of any special upcoming events. If these notices were printed on your letterhead, you would have the dual advantage of notifying them about the event and informing them that you are in the real estate business and giving the name of your company and the phone number and address where they can reach you.

Does the organization have a new-member welcoming committee? It is always difficult to become comfortable in a new group of people. Many organizations have a new-member welcoming committee. The purpose of this committee is to alleviate some of the anxieties of its newer members. Members of this committee will serve at new-member parties or receptions that are held at regular intervals during the year, or they may be called upon to visit new members in their homes. These new people are, of course, grateful for the kindnesses extended to them by the members of this committee. Because many of these new members are probably corporate transferees, they will most likely be transferring out of town in the next two or three years. The help you give them in becoming comfortable could make you the number-one candidate to list their home when they have to make the move out of the area again. If your organization does not have such a new-member committee, start one.

I hope that this religious-group example has helped clarify the techniques available to you when using social farming as a meaningful tool in promoting yourself. If you are now considering or may later consider social farming in a particular group, ask yourself the questions that we explored in the religious-group situation. If the answers are favorable in your target group, go for it.

Remember, however, to make a plan of how you will develop this group. Regardless of the details of your plan, it must portray you as a helpful, valuable member of the group and not simply a self-serving one.

GEOGRAPHIC FARMING

Geographic farming is a real estate selling concept that is often discussed but seldom implemented successfully. Simply stated, it involves targeting a specific group of homes for a strong personal promotion program by a salesperson. This is done for the purpose of winning the loyalty of all the homeowners in this area through a constant and continuous program of reminders that you are successful in their neighborhood. After repetitive exposure to you and your successes, homeowners begin to seek you out when it is time to list their homes for sale.

This technique, like all others described here, calls for commitment and self-discipline on the part of the salesperson in order to realize significant results. If this technique is implmented with imagination and consistency, it can propel you into big earnings and wreak havoc with the competition.

The key to success in geographic farming is to select an area that gives you the best chance to enhance the results of your efforts.

The factors to consider in selecting the best area include:

• What is the number of homes in the area?
• What are the backgrounds of the area residents?
• What is the amount of turnover in home sales?
• What is the economic outlook for the future of the area?
• What is the severity of the competition?

What is the number of homes in the area? You must get a count of the number of homes in the area you are considering. What is the total market? How costly will a mailing program be if you want to send something to each homeowner from time to time? How long will it take for you to see each homeowner in person? Some geographic farms have a total of 200 homes while others have more than 2,000 homes.

What are the backgrounds of the area residents? Will the homeowners in this area relate to you? Will you have something in common with them? Will they feel comfortable with you and you with them? Do you have the same educational background? Do you also live in the area and enjoy the amenities it has to offer its residents? Do you send your children to the same schools as most area homeowners? The basic question being asked really deals with the comfort level that these owners will have with you as a person. We all like to do business with people who have our best interests at heart. If you share something in common with the majority of the area's residents, the odds are that you will succeed in winning their confidence in you.

What is the amount of turnover in home sales? How many homes sell in this area each year? You must go to your multiple listing service (M.L.S.) information and find out how many homes were sold in the last 12 months. Let's assume, for example, that you find that 30 homes were sold in this area last year and that the average price was $70,000 on each sale. The total sales volume was $70,000 × 30 = $2,100,000 for an entire year. You must now ask yourself how much sales volume you need in order to justify the investment in time and expense to develop this farm. If you are looking for a minimum of $1 million in sales volume from the farm you choose, it would mean that you would have to get just about 50 percent of all the sales made last year to achieve your goal. I don't believe you should choose an area if you must do more than 25 percent of all sales to make the amount of money that you want to earn. So, in this example, this area would have needed 60 sales a year at the average sales price of $70,000 before it could fit your parameters of 25 percent minimum and $1 million in sales volume.

What is the economic outlook for the future of the area? If home prices are going down in the area you are considering, it will be a difficult area to work successfully. The area's existing homeowners will be more difficult to negotiate with because they are not working with large profit margins. They may put a lot of pressure on you to reduce your brokerage fee to help them realize the net proceeds that they want from the sale. It will also be more difficult to get the listings sold because buyers will be hesitant to invest in an area where they feel that their newly bought home may go down in value. If someone does make an offer, they will probably want a substantial discount from today's value as a hedge against the future. This, in turn, will make it all the more difficult for you to bring buyer and seller to mutually agreeable terms.

On the other hand, if home prices are rising, the opposite is true. Sellers are making profits when they sell and are less likely to squabble over brokerage fees. Buyers are more anxious to buy homes in this area because they feel that their newly purchased home will increase in value over the period that they enjoy its use.

What is the severity of the competition? When gathering the M.L.S. data on sales, pay particular attention to the listing broker and listing salesperson on each sale. If you see the same one or two names often, it would behoove you to find out what percentage of all sales in the area these one or two people are currently doing. If there is a strong salesperson who has 25 percent or more of the market, you will have to evaluate your chances of succeeding against someone who obviously has begun developing this farm ahead of you. Yes, it is possible to beat a well-entrenched competitor. But you will have to weigh the expense in terms of time, cost, and energy to see if it is worth the effort on your part.

The ideal geographic farm for you will be a size that you can handle from a cost-and-time standpoint. It will be comprised of homeowners who share a common bond with you. It will have an adequate number of sales each year so that you can realize your financial goals without having to get more than 25 percent of all sales. The value of homes in the area should be on the increase and the market should not be dominated by one competing salesperson with a 25 percent market share or greater.

When you begin to get results in a geographic farm, you must dramatize your success in order to gain additional listings. The most dramatic thing I ever did is shown on page 67. The dots shown on the map represent each of my listings that were sold. Nothing impresses people more than your results in their neighborhood. Consider using a visual aid similar to this when you think the timing is right.

TWELVE SUCCESSFUL STRATEGIES

Now that we have explored the two basic farming concepts, social and geographic, we can examine 12 time-proven strategies that can be implemented as part of a farming program. They can also stand alone as career-building techniques. They are:

1. Personal canvassing
2. For-sale-by-owners
3. Expired listings of other brokers
4. Personal brochures
5. Personal promotion
6. Greeting cards
7. Just-listed/just-sold cards
8. Newsletters
9. A new-model open house
10. Good old-fashioned service
11. Getting listings by working with buyers
12. Holiday activities

As you begin to read about each of the preceding techniques and hear the success stories of people who had tremendous results, begin asking yourself which of them would be best for you. Although you will be asked to select the strategies you want to implement

LATHRUP HOMES SOLD BY TOM ERVIN ! !

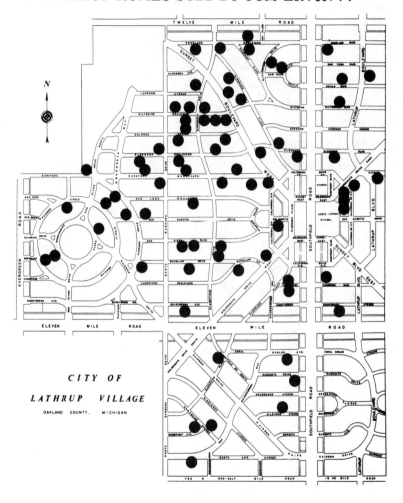

CITY OF

LATHRUP VILLAGE

OAKLAND COUNTY, MICHIGAN

in the final chapter, read each story that follows with these questions in mind:

1. Is this a strategy I can afford financially?
2. Do I have the time to use this strategy?
3. Do I have the energy to use this strategy?
4. Do I feel comfortable with this approach?
5. Will I implement this strategy consistently?
6. Does this strategy employ visual aids?
7. Will this strategy portray me as a winner?
8. Do I target the same people consistently?
9. Do I provide a unique service to my target group?

Campaign Strategy 1: *Personal Canvassing*

Personal canvassing is the practice of calling on homeowners one at a time by going up to each door and introducing yourself to them. This is always done without a prearranged appointment of any kind. Most salespeople don't like to go personally door to door. Those who do try it are usually easily discouraged and stop doing it before they have the chance for any real success.

Personal canvassing is not a quick-fix strategy. If done with some forethought and planning, however, it can and does bring long-term, lasting results. The overwhelming advantage of personal canvassing is that it puts the salesperson in face-to-face contact with a potential client. All homeowners eventually sell their home, and door-to-door calling permits the opportunity for the salesperson to build a rapport with the owner in advance of the decision to sell. If the homeowner has had the chance to meet and become comfortable with a particular salesperson, the odds are that the homeowner will choose that person to list the property as someone more familiar than a stranger.

The top reason most salespeople are not successful with personal canvassing is that they are not prepared to make a maximum impact at each home. If there is a good reason to be at the front door of a homeowner, the reception you receive will be positive. There are four good reasons for a salesperson to be at the front door of a homeowner:

1. Introducing yourself and bringing a gift.
2. Canvassing around a new listing.
3. Canvassing around an upcoming open house.
4. Canvassing around a recent sale.

Introducing yourself and bringing a gift. If you have decided to work in a specific neighborhood, the best way to become known is to get around and personally introduce yourself. Most salespeople who do this bring only a business card with them. You can increase the impact of your call by also bringing a gift of some sort, some of which might be calendars, yardsticks, cookbooks, emergency phone-number stickers, appointment books, road atlases, or any other easy-to-carry items. When purchased in large quantities, the price can be reduced to the 25- to 30-cents range.

You should, of course, always leave your business card. Be sure to have your photo printed on the card. This will enhance your chances that each homeowner will more easily remember you and recognize you the next time you meet.

When making the call, introduce yourself and explain to the homeowner that you are going to become an expert on home values, market conditions, interest rates, and any other factors that affect real estate sales in that neighborhood. Say that you have come by today to meet everyone in the neighborhood, leave your card, and bring a gift to each resident as a means of introducing yourself. This technique helps "break the ice" and serves as a good foundation for your future marketing approaches.

If your plans are to walk through an entire subdivision, don't try to do too many homes in one day. If you get overly tired the first day out, you may become discouraged and less likely to finish your plan as originally conceived. It would be better for you to call on only five homes per day if you would do it consistently and finish visiting every homeowner in your target area.

Canvassing around a new listing. There are three fantastic moments in the lives of real estate salespeople. These include getting the listing, getting the listing sold, and getting the sale to close. The attainment of a new listing is also a very important moment in the lives of the homeowners who give you the opportunity to sell their home and of the neighbors who have large investments in the success of the neighborhood.

Few salespeople go around to meet the neighbors immediately after listing a home for sale. This can be an excellent chance to sell yourself as an aggressive and hard-working salesperson. You can also render a service to your seller by soliciting the help of the neighbors to find a buyer.

When making these calls, tell the homeowners that you have just listed the home of their neighbor, Mr. and Mrs. _____. The reason you came by, you say, was to let them know that the home is now for sale, and you would like them to keep it in mind in the event that they may know of someone who may express an interest in living in their neighborhood. You also wanted them to receive your business card and keep it handy so they can call you with any leads.

The normal rule of thumb is that you should call on at least 20 homes, which would include the 5 homes on either side of and 10 across the street from the home you listed. I consider these numbers to be a minimum and recommend that you consider doubling that number if possible. Remember that people are interested in their neighborhoods, and each call gives you the opportunity to meet a future client.

Canvassing around an upcoming open house. An open house provides you with the only opportunity you have to demonstrate to the neighbors that you are actively working on behalf of your seller. When it comes time for them to choose a Realtor to list their home, they will select someone who they feel will work hard on getting their home sold. Use an upcoming open house as a rare chance to sell yourself as a dedicated and earnest representative of your seller. This is best done by going door to door a few days in advance of the open-house date.

Tell each neighbor that you will be holding the open house that Sunday between the hours of 2 P.M. and 5 P.M. If they know of someone who has expressed an interest in living in their neighborhood, you add, please contact them or let you call them to extend a personal invitation to see the house this Sunday. Thank them for their time, and remind them to call you if they hear of someone in the future who might be interested in seeing the house that is for sale.

Have you ever had a real estate salesperson come to your door in advance of holding an open house in your neighborhood? Just think of how impressed you would be by a person with that much energy and commitment to servicing that listing. You should plan on visiting at least 20 homes in advance of an open house. Remember that this technique enables you to get some help in finding a potential buyer, and it demonstrates to the entire neighborhood that you are the kind of salesperson who should represent them in the sale of their own home when the time comes.

Canvassing around a recent sale. The neighbors are, of course, curious when a home is newly listed and a for-sale sign first appears on a neighborhood front lawn. They are also impressed when you come around to see them in advance of an open house, but nothing can compare with the news that the house is sold. It is news that is discussed around the dinner tables of many neighbors the day the "sold" sign goes up. For you, the listing salesperson, it is more than news; it is a personal victory.

It is also a victory for each homeowner in the immediate neighborhood. When a home sells, each homeowner knows that more people are still interested in investing in their neighborhood. They also feel a little more comfortable that they will be able to find a buyer for their home when they decide to sell. If it was a quick sale, this is even more proof that there is strong demand for homes in the area.

You should visit as many neighbors as you can around the time of a recent sale. We are all impressed with those who can get results. Use a recent sale to your advantage by giving out the good news in person. If, however, you have already visited the neighbors at the time of the listing or of open house, send them a "just-sold" card, giving your name and the number of days the house was on the market.

Personal Canvassing Success Story:
Dee Amsler
H.E.R. Realtors
Columbus, Ohio

The story you are about to read is one of the most dramatic examples of the devastating power of a marketing program well conceived and consistently executed with painstaking exactness and attention to detail. Dee Amsler, of Columbus, Ohio, entered the real estate business in September of 1976 with no prior selling experience. In 1984 she took three months off to go sailing with her husband in their 37-foot Irwin sailboat. During 1984 she sold nearly $6.5 million in real estate.

Approximately 80 percent of her business comes from listings sold in a 325-home geographic farm that she has developed for the past eight years. She has a part-time secretary who operates the Digital Equipment Corporation computer Dee has purchased to handle her high-volume needs. Dee's computer stores a wealth of information on her farm area, and it permits her great versatility in keeping in contact with her clients. To make the story even more incredible, Dee and her family had only lived in Columbus for three weeks before she began her real estate career.

How can someone with no prior sales experience, living in an unfamiliar city, reach such astounding heights of achievement? Like every other real-life success story, it wasn't easy, and there were disappointments along the way.

Because she was new and eager to learn, she listened to the advice given by her broker. The advice was to get out and canvass door to door. If she did this, she was told that she would succeed. In 1977 she began calling on her neighbors in the new-home subdivision in which she lived. Because the builders were still selling more new homes in the subdivision, her original neighborhood contained only 60 homes.

As she went door to door, she gave each homeowner a copy of a newsletter she had composed. It contained the prices the builders were getting for the new homes they were selling. This enabled each homeowner to compare what they had paid for their model versus what they were selling for currently. She did this every other month for 18 months with no results. This was largely due to the fact that all the present homeowners had not lived there long, and the normal turnover had not yet begun.

In 1978 the subdivision had 120 homes, and finally in 1979 it had grown to a completed number of 325 homes. Because of her regular delivery of the newsletter, the neighbors became dependent on reading the information she had compiled for them. She could see that the homeowners appreciated it when she provided community-oriented services that made their lives in the subdivision more enjoyable.

She was one of the founders of the civic association in the subdivision that appointed a captain on each block to help new people get the answers they needed and gave information about upcoming events. She bought a Santa Claus suit for the annual Christmas party. She donated $50 to be used as prize money at the annual Halloween party for the kids with the scariest or funniest costumes. She hand delivered to each home a card with emergency phone numbers and the name and phone number of the local block captain.

Also in 1977 H.E.R. Realtors began publishing a cookbook to be given out door to door as a gift to homeowners. Dee gave these out in her subdivision and is still doing this once each year when it is published.

In 1978 the homes began to come up for sale. Early in the year she got her first listing in the subdivision. She sold the house, received a referral to the homeowner's friend, and sold four homes in a two-month period. By the end of 1978 she had earned approximately $8,500 from the subdivision.

Because all the homes were now occupied, Dee decided to change the format of her newsletter. Instead of giving the prices of recent sales, she began, in 1979, to include the latest interest rates, other market information, and the number of homes under contract that were awaiting a closing date.

Beginning in 1980 she switched from delivering the newsletter every other month to delivering it on a quarterly schedule. About this time the civic association, with Dee's help, decided to publish a directory of all the residents in the subdivision. This directory contained the names of all homeowners including their children's names, ages, and any odd jobs the children would do, such as baby-sitting and lawn cutting. It also listed the deed restrictions that pertained to the subdivision as well as the annual schedule of events such as a hayride and Easter egg hunt. Dee paid for the entire production and printing of the directory, which cost $1,300. She had 425 directories printed so that she would have extra copies to give to the new families who moved in. Because she paid for it, she also had her name imprinted on the cover.

H.E.R. Realtors, Dee's company, began printing a company newsletter in 1981. She distributed this one in addition to her own by putting it in a plastic bag and leaving it on each door knob on Saturdays.

Of course, Dee is not without competitors. In 1979

she had 13 full-time REALTORS® living in the same subdivision. This number grew to 19 in 1982. They saw what Dee was doing, and they also took to the sidewalks with a door-to-door campaign. One of these competitors, in particular, began getting a few listings.

In an effort to stop any further inroads by this competitor, Dee came up with yet another unique service to offer to the residents. She had a clown suit made for her married daughter, and she purchased party favors in quantity. These included hats, noisemakers, and helium-filled balloons. She then sent a flyer to all the residents announcing that she would provide upon advance notice a clown and party favors for a birthday party for any children 12 years or younger. These parties cost her about $20 apiece. They were much talked about and widely used by the homeowners, and once again, Dee had dramatically improved her visibility in the neighborhood.

In 1982 she made approximately $23,000 from the contacts she had built in the subdivision. In 1983 her income reached $55,000 from the sale of her listings there and the referrals from people living in the subdivision.

Now she gets around the subdivision in person twice each year because of the time invested in closing and processing her large volume of sales. When she takes her newsletter, she includes a little card that invites the homeowner to submit a recipe that may be used in the next issue of the cookbook.

As if all the things Dee does aren't enough, she performs two other routines that lock her domination of the subdivision up tight:

1. She has created a book that contains a photo of each of the 325 homes in her geographic farm. Under each photo she writes down the date and selling price every time there is a sale. When she goes on a listing presentation, she does not need any extra preparation because all the facts are in her book. Can you imagine the impact on a potential seller when Dee opens her book and shows him or her photographs and selling prices on every home in the subdivision including their own home?

2. Dee drives through her farm regularly with a notebook and pen. She writes down the address of any property on which work is being done, such as an addition, painting, paving, landscaping, or any other noticeable change. When she gets a call of any kind from a resident of the subdivision, she asks the caller what his or her address is and she says, "Oh, you had new shutters put on your house last spring." Such a comment always amazes the caller and instantly installs her as the unequalled expert in her area.

Her actual earnings for years 1976 through 1982 were as follows:

1976	$ 0
1977	3,200
1978	8,500
1979	13,000
1980	17,000
1981	21,000+
1982	23,000+

Dee's earnings in 1983 and 1984 were well into six figures from farm-area business and referrals originated by residents of the farm.

Very few of us approach our careers with the intensity and commitment of Dee Amsler. From this amazing story, however, you should pick out those techniques that appeal to you and design a similar program that can enable you to earn a six-figure income with three months off for good behavior.

Obviously, Dee spent a lot of time, effort, and money in her farming program. You do not have to do all the things she did in order to be successful at geographic farming. Start with the simple things:

- Send an introductory letter to each homeowner with your photo on the letter and enclosing a business card.
- Begin going door to door while leaving some gift item such as a calendar or inexpensive cookbook.
- Call on the for-sale-by-owners and expired listings in the farm.
- Send out just-listed and just-sold cards when the occasion presents itself.

Keep up your visibility and stay in touch. Your consistency will pay off. If you have a creative bent and would like to use some original ideas of your own, do it.

Personal Canvassing Success Story:
Joe

Jamie O'Neill, Inc. Realtors

Oklahoma City, Oklahoma

I don't remember his last name. It has been almost 20 years since I met him back in the mid-sixties. I do recall his simple method of canvassing a subdivision. I still remember it because it was a plan that anyone could do. I was introduced to Joe because he was the top salesperson in the two-office company I was visiting. When I asked him how he became the top person, he related his technique.

He targeted a 400-home subdivision that was between his home and his office. Each day he would drive to the subdivision at 9 A.M. He would go to the doors of five homes and introduce himself to the five homeowners. Upon meeting each homeowner, he would explain that he was specializing in homes in their neighborhood, and he wanted to meet each resident in order to let people know who he was.

After calling on the five people, he would drive to his office where he addressed five preprinted letters to the people he had met that morning. The letters thanked the homeowners for letting him meet them and reminded them that he was specializing in their area. After putting them on the secretary's desk to be mailed, he was finished with his program for the day.

The total daily elapsed time was one hour. He did this five days each week. At five homes per day, he met 100 homeowners a month and the entire subdivision in four months. He walked through that subdivision three times a year.

Every time he took another lap around the 400 homes, he became more familiar with the subdivision. His letters began talking about his listing-and-selling success in the neighborhood. People began seeing his "for sale" and "sold" signs popping up. The neighbors began to talk among themselves about how hard working and successful Joe was. His name became a household word, and those 400 families formed the nucleus for all his future sales successes.

Joe's story is a tribute to a little creativity and a lot of consistency and commitment to implementing a good idea.

This method was not costly, took little time each day, and produced dramatic results. Consider doing the same thing. It would not take you very long to get started. Just pick your area, start calling on five homes a day, and write your letters and make copies.

Campaign Strategy 2: *For-Sale-by-Owners*

Every selling profession has a difficult time finding leads for new business. Real estate sales is a notable exception to that rule. Not only do people tell us they need our services, they actually spend their own money to put us on notice. They go out and buy a for-sale sign for the front yard, and they buy a classified ad in the local newspaper telling us about their problem and how to get in touch with them. No real estate salesperson should ever be at a loss for new business leads. Most salespeople do try to cultivate the for-sale-by-owner lead at some point in their career. Very few do it successfully.

It's not easy. Frankly, the for-sale-by-owner (f.s.b.o.), provides us with a classic confrontation: Here we have a homeowner who is announcing to the world that he or she does not want to pay for the services of a Realtor. In the other corner is the Realtor who works on commission and whose sole livelihood depends on convincing people to list their homes and agree to pay a fee for the Realtor's services.

The reason most salespeople do not succeed with f.s.b.o.s is that they deal with the homeowner in a confrontational manner. We say things like, "I see you're trying to sell your home" or "Welcome to the real estate business." These kinds of comments only tend to heighten emotions and make the homeowner more determined than ever to avoid real estate people. The best way to persuade a f.s.b.o. to list his or her home with you is to get the owner's emotions working for you rather than against you. I will propose three techniques that have worked very well for me when trying to win over a f.s.b.o.

The four-postcard approach. I don't believe in using the telephone to try to get an appointment with a f.s.b.o. I realize there are salespeople who do get results with the phone, but I think most homeowners selling their home themselves are deluged with real estate people calling them at all hours of the day or night. I don't want to be another nameless, faceless stranger on the other end of the telephone line. I always prefer a different approach from my competition. This four-postcard approach enabled me to list 50 percent of f.s.b.o.s I went after in seven years of selling. As a matter of fact, this technique launched my career in real estate and was the greatest source of my income in the first critical year of venturing into commission sales.

The four-postcard approach is based on the premise that most people admire creativity, that they like consistency, and that they have a sense of humor. I cut a f.s.b.o. ad out of the paper and taped it to a 3″ × 5″ card. I then addressed four postcards. The cards read as follows:

1. TOM ERVIN CAN . . .
2. TOM ERVIN CAN SELL YOUR HOME . . .
3. TOM ERVIN CAN SELL YOUR HOME QUICKER AT HIGHEST PRICE BECAUSE . . .

4. TOM ERVIN CAN SELL YOUR HOME QUICKER AT HIGHEST PRICE BECAUSE I AM JUST AS PERSISTENT IN FINDING BUYERS AS I WAS IN SENDING YOU THIS MAILING!

You will notice, also, that my photo grew from one-quarter size to full size in the fourth card (see page 87). This added a little suspense, to find out what I looked like. My f.s.b.o. received these cards one at a time over a four-day period. On the evening of the fifth day, I appeared at the homeowners' front door. When they came to the door, I gave my best smile and said, "I bet you can't guess who I am!" This always brought a laugh and an admission that they knew very well who I was because they had been reading my postcards for the last four days. They used to talk about me at dinner while wondering when and how they would hear from me in person. After the fourth day, I had become fixed in their minds as a creative and unique saleperson who was not like all the others who kept bothering them on the telephone. I never invited myself into the house on that first visit. I simply told them that it was a pleasure to meet them in person after corresponding with them through the mail all week, and I wished them success in selling their home. Sometimes they would invite me in on that initial call and other times not. I always returned to their front door each week thereafter on the same week-night until their home was listed or sold. Each time I returned I brought them some tidbit of news that was helpful to them. These news items would

Tom
Ervin
can . . .

Tom Ervin
can
sell your home . .

Tom Ervin
can
sell your home
quicker at highest
price because . . .

Tom Ervin can sell your
home quicker at highest
price because . . . I am just as
persistent in finding buyers
as I was in sending you this
mailing!

THE COMPANY, REALTORS

include recent sales in the neighborhood, price changes on competing homes, and the latest interest rates. We usually became friends over this period because our first face-to-face meeting began with a laugh, and I remained as a helpful and consistently friendly ally.

You could have similar postcards printed with your photo and message at any quick-print store. The blank postcards can be purchased at your local post office.

The homeowner's survival kit. Another concept that worked very well was something called the homeowner's survival kit. It was similar to the postcards in that it relied on humor as its main ingredient. I would go to the local drugstore and purchase envelopes that looked like legal files. They were the size of a regular #10 envelope, but they had an accordion fold on the bottom and an elastic band that would securely hold the contents inside. I would put a sample purchase agreement, a brochure on how to show your home successfully, and two aspirin tablets in the envelope. On the front side, I had a label that read in bold letters, "The Homeowner's Survival Kit."

With the envelope in hand, I would walk unannounced up to the front door of a f.s.b.o. at about 7 P.M. When the homeowners appeared, I would introduce myself and explain that I knew selling a home wasn't easy and I brought something that might help. I would then show them my survival kit. After opening it, I would first remove the purchase agreement while saying that I wanted them to have a legally binding document to use when signing up their buyer.

I also wanted them to have a little brochure that would give them some good ideas on how to show their home to its best advantage. Last, I said, I knew selling a home could be a headache at times and I wanted them to have two aspirin tablets close by when those times arose. They always enjoyed this approach, were appreciative of the purchase agreement and brochure, and were amused by the aspirin tablets and survival kit.

Here again, my first meeting with them was humorous, relaxed, and nonconfrontational. As with the postcard approach, I continued visiting these f.s.b.o.s each week on the same week-night, providing them with helpful tidbits of news until they either sold the house themselves or listed it.

Only two things happen. This third method can also be successful without any of the advance planning necessary with the other two approaches. In this example, you go to the front door, introduce yourself, give the owner your card and say, "I see you are selling your home yourself." The owner will always reply with something like, "Yes, we are selling it ourselves. We are not going to use a Realtor."

To this, you respond, "I understand and I wish you good luck in selling your home. I came by this evening to introduce myself and share with you that it has been my experience that only two things happen. Either the owner is successful in selling his or her own home and toward that end I wish you well, or the owner chooses to use the services of a Realtor. These are the only two things that can happen." (While giving this explanation, it is more effective if you are holding two fingers up so you can dramatize the number two.) "If you do choose in the future to seek the services of a Realtor, I would appreciate it if you would give me the opportunity to show you my marketing plan for your home. Thank you and good evening."

As in the other methods, you should return to the front door of this homeowner on the same week-night each succeeding week until the home is sold or listed. Remember to bring some helpful tidbits of news that will be of interest to these owners.

National statistics tell us that only 8 percent of all f.s.b.o.s are successful in selling their home without the services of a Realtor. Only one out of 12 is going to make it on his or her own. The odds are in favor of the salesperson who uses a unique approach and persists with face-to-face encounters until the owner finally decides to throw in the towel. Stick with it. Remember, the odds are in your favor.

Don't try these f.s.b.o. techniques unless you are prepared also to go back each week for the follow-up calls. It usually takes two or three such calls to build the kind of personal rapport that you want.

Bring some item of news that will help the homeowners learn something they did not know about the market as it affects the salability of their home. They will appreciate it, and you can win them over with your consistency, kindnesses, and real estate knowledge.

Campaign Strategy 3: *Expired Listings of Other Brokers*

More than 50 percent of all properties listed with a Realtor will go unsold in the original listing period. This happens for a variety of reasons depending on the individual circumstances. The reasons usually are, however, that the home is overpriced or that the listing agent did not service the listing in a manner sufficient enough to give it the proper market exposure it deserved.

Human nature being what it is, most homeowners blame the listing agent for the fact that their house is not sold. The next time you pick up your M.L.S. book filled with current listings, remember that 50 percent of them will be up for grabs when they expire.

Here we have a homeowner who is agreeable to paying a real estate fee for results. He or she is a well-qualified prospect. As in other approaches, the creative and dramatic idea will stand out in the owner's mind. I suggest two methods. The first of these is the letter that follows:

Dear Property Owner,

Have you ever wondered why some properties sell right away, at top prices, while others never seem to sell at any price? The answer is quite simple! Statistics show that 75 percent of all real estate is sold by 25 percent of all sales associates. The trick is to get one of these people selling your property.

A good salesperson has a "plan of action" and follows

through with it. Enclosed, please find my "plan of action" with its 21 points.

_____ has some of the top salespeople in this area! We sell over _____ million dollars in real estate every month in this area alone.

I would consider it a privilege to be of assistance to you. I have been full time in the real estate business for _____ years and am one of the 25 percent. Please call me for a profitable experience.

I am looking forward to meeting you and selling your property.

Sincerely,

_____
Bus. phone _____
Home phone _____

THE PLAN OF ACTION

Our company objectives are the following:
1. To get as many *qualified* buyers as possible into your home until it is SOLD
2. To *communicate* the results of our activities weekly to you
3. To assist you in getting the *highest possible dollar value* for your property with the least number of problems
4. To constantly look for the best possible methods of exposing your property to the potential buyers in the market

The following is our company's plan for marketing your home:

1. Submit your home to the Multiple Listing Service
2. Submit copies of your listing to our company sales staff for their waiting buyers
3. Tour your home with my office staff
4. Promote your home at the Real Estate Board meetings for maximum exposure to the other agents in the area

5. Develop a list of features and benefits of your home for the cooperating agents to use with their potential buyers
6. Suggest and advise you as to any changes you might want to make on your property to make it even more marketable to the buyer
7. Keep you up-to-date regarding any changes in the market, both in prices and change in the money market and their effects on the sale of your property
8. Knock on 50 doors in the surrounding area
9. Provide additional exposure through a professional sign and lock box
10. Hold an open house when possible
11. Advertise for specific buyers regularly
12. Pre-qualify when possible all prospective buyers
13. Make you completely aware of all the various methods of financing that your buyer may want to use
14. Have the cooperating brokers in your area tour your home
15. Provide on a monthly basis for the cooperating brokers a list of the features and benefits of your home
16. Follow up on all the salespeople who have shown your home for their response
17. Assist you in arranging interim financing, if necessary
18. Deliver a copy of your multiple listing for your approval, also a copy of all advertisements that have been published
19. Represent you upon the presentation of all contracts by the cooperating brokers and help in negotiating the best possible price and terms for you
20. Handle follow-up and keep you informed, after the contract has been accepted, on all mortgage, title, and other closing procedures
21. Deliver your check at the closing

Submitted by   Your Acknowledgment

_____

This letter and action plan should be mailed to an expired listing immediately upon expiration or as soon as you can determine that a listing has expired. It has been successfully used in obtaining hundreds of listings in the past 10 years. Send out lots of them. Remember that it is a numbers game.

Another imaginative approach has involved the use of a professional résumé or application for employment. When a listing expires, the homeowner must decide whom to hire for the desired results the second time around. Why not use a new approach through the use of an application for employment? It is different, unique, and certain to catch the attention of its recipient. Most salespeople send a simple letter or make a phone call. The application for employment denotes a desire to be hired and a willingness to go to work.

Eric Olson, its originator, was successful in securing numerous expired listings. He found it particularly effective in soliciting absentee owners of expired listings. His credentials, photo, and unique approach provided enough reason to pick up the phone and hire Eric as the next listing agent.

APPLICATION FOR EMPLOYMENT

PERSONAL INFORMATION:

Name:	Eric J. Olson, G.R.I.
Residence Address:	240 Bowdoinhill, Rochester, MI
Office Address:	127 W. University, Rochester, MI

EMPLOYMENT DESIRED:

Position:	Exclusive Marketing Representative for your home
Date Available:	Available Immediately

PROFESSIONAL EXPERIENCE: Real Estate One, Inc., Associate Broker
Five Years of real estate experience in residential and commercial sales and leasing.

Real Estate Securities Agent
The Syndications Corporation
Kalamazoo, Michigan

PROFESSIONAL TRAINING: Graduate, Realtors Institutes I, II, & III
Real Estate Securities & Syndication Institute's Course 501 & 601
Numerous investment & real estate educational seminars.

PROFESSIONAL DESIGNATIONS & AWARDS: Graduate, Realtors Institute
Distinguished Service Award, Pontiac Jaycees.

PROFESSIONAL AFFILIATIONS: Rochester Board of Realtors
Michigan Association of Realtors
National Association of Realtors

EDUCATION: Walsh College, Troy, Michigan (Student)
University of Michigan, B.A., Ann Arbor, MI 1973
Northwestern Michigan College, Traverse City, MI

REMARKS: Since you are, in fact, employing a salesperson when you sell your home, it might be a good idea to have them complete an application.

My success formula is Personal Service, Professionalism, Market Knowledge and Aggressive Advertising.

Now that you know who I am, let me go to work for you!

CALL TODAY AND ASK FOR ERIC J. OLSON.

Thank you,

Eric J. Olson

Eric J. Olson

Office Phone: 652-6500
Residence: 375-9712

Real Estate One, Inc.
Michigan's Largest Real Estate Company

Expired Listings Success Story:
Madeline Hayes
Goodman, Segar, Hogan Realtors
Virginia Beach, Virginia

Madeline Hayes is a recent arrival in the real estate business, but she has all the moves and the results of a proven professional. In her first 12 months, she sold $2.5 million in real estate despite the fact that she had no prior selling experience.

The most amazing part of this story is that 70 percent of her volume comes from a detailed system of getting other brokers' expired listings. Most salespeople don't feel confident trying to obtain expired listings, yet Madeline enjoys it and has become extremely good at it.

Her system has several steps that lead up to the successful attainment of a listing:

1. Each month, she goes through the current multiple-listing book looking for those listings that have one more month to go until expiration.
2. She then narrows the listings she will pursue to a list of 10 target properties. In order to qualify for the list, a property must have had some problem that she could correct once she became the listing agent. Some of these correctable problems are:
   a. An attractive home without a lock box
   b. A listing agent who gives poor service
   c. A seller who has not been instructed to offer any financing terms to attract buyers
   d. A large but overpriced equity position
   e. No changes in price or terms since home was originally listed indicating a lack of good communication between the current listing agent and the seller.
3. Now that the 10 target listings have been identified, she makes appointments to preview each property when the seller is home.
4. Madeline begins continually checking the M.L.S. computer each day to see if any of her target properties expired the previous night. When she sees one of them on the expired list, she immediately calls the owner. She reminds the owner of her recent visit and sets an appointment to discuss her marketing plan for the property.

5. She is usually competing with three or four other people on each listing. During the presentation, she uses the following strategy:
    a. First sells herself as an individual and shows her sales statistics
    b. Reviews how the listing was marketed in the past and recommends changes
    c. Takes a tour of the house, explaining to the owners that she is going to view the house the same way a critical buyer would look at it, and then makes suggestions regarding potential improvements in decor and appearance.

Through this detailed and well-planned process, Madeline secures the listing on 4 out of 10 properties targeted each month. Remember that these are not just any four properties. These homes and their selling potential were analyzed in some depth before she ever went after them. She was confident she could make some adjustments in the price, terms, condition, availability for showings, or communication with the seller that would assure her of a sale during her listing period.

Her $2.5 million in sales volume achieved during her first 12 months in the real estate business bears testimony to the effectiveness of her efforts.

The expired-listing success story just described assumes that you are able to obtain expiration dates through your multiple listing service. If expiration dates are not readily available, you can still use

Madeline's method. What is the average listing period in your area? Is it 90 days? 120 days? How many listings have been processed by your M.L.S. in each of the last few months?

If you can find the answers to the preceding questions, do the following:

1. Multiple listing services assign a sequential number to each listing. Go to you M.L.S. statistics and see how many listings were taken during each of the last four months.
2. Let's assume that the average listing period in your area is 120 days. Let's also assume that today is the first day of the month of May. Look at the first M.L.S. number you receive today. Let's say it is number 13,400.
3. Assume the following:
   Listings taken in April—500
   Subtracting 500 from 13,400 tells us that the numbers 12,900 through 13,399 were listed in the month of April. That group will be expiring in the month of August.

   Listings taken in March—700
   Subtracting 700 from 12,900 tells us that the numbers 12,200 through 12,899 were listed in the month of March. That group will be expiring in July.

   Listings taken in February—400
   Subtracting 400 from 12,200 tells us that the numbers 11,800 through 12,199 were listed in February

and will be expiring in June.

Listings taken in January—300
Subtracting 300 from 11,800 tells us that the numbers 11,500 through 11,799 were listed in January and will be expiring in the present month of May.
4. Go through your current M.L.S. book looking for listings with any number between 11,500 and 11,799. If they meet the criteria used by Madeline, pick 10 as your target properties for the month of May. You have also identified those that will be expiring for the four months following.
5. To determine the exact expiration date, keep checking the M.L.S. computer each day for the current status of each of your 10 target properties. When the computer shows a listing as no longer current, it has just expired the previous night.

This method should work in any area.

Campaign Strategy 4: *The Personal Brochure*

The old selling adage tells us that people must first be sold on the salesperson before they will be in the proper frame of mind to buy whatever the salesperson is trying to sell. This is especially true in the real estate business.

So many of us have real estate licenses. Hundreds of new people in the United States are becoming licensed every month. All of us have one thing in common. We all use a business card to introduce ourselves and to leave with people as a reminder of our name, company affiliation, address, and phone number. How ordinary!

Some salespeople are using an item that either replaces a business card or is given out with a business card. This item is called a personal brochure. As the name implies, it is a brochure. This brochure does not sell a seminar, a product, or a service. It sells you, the individual sales associate.

Although the format of individual brochures may vary from one person to another depending on personal preference, most of them will include the following:

1. A photo of the sales associate
2. Educational background
3. Memberships
4. Licenses
5. Sales achievements
6. Personal philosophy

7. Testimonials
8. Name, address, company affiliation, phone number

In order for the buying and selling public to pick you out of the crowd, they must feel that you have some personal quality that makes you the perfect choice to handle their real estate needs. Effective design and use of a personal brochure can make you unique in the reader's mind.

Personal Brochure Success Story:
Elly Engberg
Realty World, Heritage, Inc.
Detroit Lakes, Minnesota

After more than three years of selling radio ads, Elly Engberg was persuaded to join a local real estate company in Detroit Lakes, Minnesota, a town with a population of 7,500 people. Elly began her first day on June 4, 1979. On June 5, 1979, mortgage interest rates went up to 11 percent and continued upward to 18 percent by March 1980.

All she heard from the other real estate people was bad news concerning a future with high rates. Having left a job where she earned approximately $40,000 per year, she became anxious about her ability to earn as much in the current real estate climate. Nevertheless, she set a personal goal for herself to equal that amount in her first year.

As is true with every top producer, Elly looked at her predicament and decided on a unique approach. Although home prices had traditionally risen in previous years, Elly decided that the sellers would be able to counter high interest rates only by reducing their prices. Other real estate salespeople said she was crazy and that people would not stand for it.

She stuck to her guns, however, and after working 72-hour weeks, she did sell $2 million worth of real estate in her first full year. In 1980–1981, she sold another $2 million. In 1981–1982, she sold $2.5 million. These volumes are particularly impressive considering that the average sale price was in the $40,000 to $50,000 range.

It was in 1982 that Elly first heard about the idea of a personal brochure while attending a Certified Residential Specialist (C.R.S.) course. After hearing of the many benefits of a personal brochure, she came home and produced the brochure shown on page 106. She had 1,000 brochures printed and used them in the following ways:

1. She sent them to out-of-town sellers of both for-sale-by-owner and expired listings along with a letter.
2. She gave them out in every situation where she would usually hand out a business card.
3. She gave them to friends and customers.

4. She always carried a supply in her car, to be given to local merchants where she traded.
5. She gave them out at meetings she attended.
6. She gave them out door to door in target areas.
7. She gave them to out-of-town real estate people to encourage them to send her referrals.

Elly felt it was important to be different from other salespeople, and the brochure helped her both to be unique and to help people understand her personal philosophy of professional service.

The year 1982 was a great one for Elly though it was the worst year in decades for the real estate industry as a whole. In the Realty World Upper Midwest Region, Elly attained the following recognition:

1. She was among the top ten listers in March, April, June, and July.
2. She was among the top ten sales leaders in April, July, and August.
3. She came in number two in listings in all of 1982.

On the local scene, she had the honor of selling 20 percent of the entire annual volume done by all members of her multiple listing service.

Like many top producers, Elly has been creative in using other marketing tools. She has been written up in her local paper for creating a three-way exchange of homes between three local property owners. She has also created "The Real Estate Guide" which is published five times each year. This 50-page photo book is

"...Our thanks to Elly for her outstanding efforts in unsnarling the tangle of "Red Tape" and loose ends in the purchase of our home. Thanks to her for her persistence and expertise...and more importantly, her personal attention."

Bob & Sue Nelson
Vergas, Mn.

"In today's real estate market, it takes a good deal of knowledge, skill and dedication to be successful in bringing buyers and sellers together. But for these fine qualities Elly brought to bear on our transaction, the purchase might have fallen through,......I look forward to working with her again in the future."
Peter Gabor
Gabor Trucking, Inc.
Detroit Lakes, Mn.

"We are more than satisfied with the three-way trade that was involved to sell our home in D.L. and buy one here in Slayton. We are glad Elly had the ingenuity to come up with this plan and then the commitment to follow it through to the end. We appreciate all the effort."
Randy & Karen Beers
Slayton, Mn.

KNOW YOUR REALTOR......

REALTY WORLD.
Heritage

......ELLY ENGBERG

QUALIFICATIONS...........

Education:

REAL ESTATE EDUCATION COMPANY
Real Estate I

WADENA AREA VO-TECH
Real Estate II

MINN. ASSN. OF REALTORS
Real Estate III
Graduate Realtors Institute Course 1-2-3
Real Estate Exchange Analysis
Advertising Real Estate
Age of Real Estate Securities
Residential Investments

UNIVERSITY OF MINN.
Contract for Deed Financing

REALTY WORLD
Listing Course
Calculator Course
Investors Finance Course
Homebuyers Finance Course
Homebuyers Finance Course Instructor Training

REALTORS NATIONAL MARKETING INSTITUTE
RS 101 Advance Listing Practice
RS 102 Advance Selling Practice

Member:

National Association of Realtors
Minnesota Association of Realtors
Detroit Lakes Board of Realtors
Detroit Lakes Board of Realtors, director 1981-82
Realtors National Marketing Institute
Minn. CRS Chapter Realtors National Marketing Institute
Graduate Realtors Institute of Minnesota
Detroit Lakes Chamber of Commerce

Licenses:

Minnesota Real Estate License 1979
North Dakota Real Estate License 1979

Awards:

Over 2 million dollars production 1980
Over 2 million dollars production 1981
REALTY WORLD Upper Midwest Region
Top 10 Award for Listing, March 1982
Top 10 Award for Production, April 1982

WHY ELLY?......

There's a lot more to selling a home than putting up a sign and running an ad in the paper. There's a lot more to buying a home than looking in the paper and driving around until you see one you like. It takes knowledge of the current housing market and up to the minute information on all types of real estate financing available. It takes careful planning to insure the Seller of the "best possible price" AND terms that will provide the Seller with enough "Hard Cash" to carry out future plans. It takes careful planning to insure the Buyer that they will financially qualify for the home they choose.

Selling and buying a home is a complex task that should be entrusted to a professional with integrity, training, experience and proven performance. Elly Engberg IS such a professional. Thoroughly trained in every phase of the real estate business, she knows the ins-and-outs on everything from planning sales strategy to negotiating the fine points in closing the sale, from financing and analysis of the Buyer's and Seller's closing costs to determining motivations. "She'll cover it all for you", from before the contract to after the settlement.

ELEANOR (ELLY) ENGBERG, GRI
Multi-million dollar agent

REALTY WORLD — Heritage
1219 Wash. Ave. P.O. Box 479
Detroit Lakes, Mn. 56501
218-847-4421 office
218-847-5177 Res.

OFFERING COMPLETE REAL ESTATE COUNSELING

published by her own company, of which she has been part owner, broker, and manager for the past two years. In addition to the normal photo ads, she has sold space to local merchants, which has helped finance the printing costs of the publication. She has worked hard and done many imaginative things along the way to sales success.

Some sales associates are reluctant to use a personal brochure because they feel uneasy about bragging about themselves. Elly tells her clients when she hands them a brochure that they should know all they can about her because, if chosen to represent them, she will become an important person in their lives. Like Elly, make a personal brochure on yourself and don't leave home without it.

Campaign Strategy 5: *Personal Promotion*

Probably every success story in this book is an example of personal promotion in one form or another. Personal promotion can take so many forms, however, that it is important enough to treat as a separate topic.

To use this technique effectively, you must have a clear understanding of the simple realities of building a real estate career. Real estate is a game of numbers. Your success is dependent on the number of people who know you are a winner and the number of people who choose you over everyone else to list their home for sale. The only way you can affect the number of people in these two categories is through an imaginative and consistent personal promotion campaign.

Each listing taken and each listing sold provides you with an instance of tangible success that you can use to promote yourself. Every satisfied customer can promote your winning image by telling others or writing a testimonial letter about you. Every "for sale" sign with your name attached gives vivid witness to your success.

A new concept to consider is putting your name on your open-house signs. Think of the hundreds of cars that pass by an open-house sign on a busy road and the enhanced visibility for you on the other signs within the subdivision.

Your personal statistics, such as list-to-sell ratio, total sales volume, number of units, your market-share percentage, years in the business, and other information provide additional opportunities for personal promotion. Your credentials in the community, such as years of residency, local schools attended, memberships, charitable work, or volunteer work, may also serve to enhance your personal credibility.

You have a potential following out there in your community that will respond to your promotional efforts, giving you business and referring you to others. Take the initiative and let them know why you are an outstanding person.

Personal Promotion Success Story:
Dave Wilcox
F. C. Tucker Company, Inc.
Indianapolis, Indiana

How would you like to meet a real estate salesperson who has sold a house a week for nine years? Dave Wilcox is your man.

He learned a long time ago that you should not keep your success a secret. We're talking about $4.4 million in annual sales. Like every other high-producing salesperson, Dave is very good at presenting himself in listing-and-selling situations. He has also backed up his day-to-day results with a steady nine-year program of promoting himself and his successes to a target group of people.

He currently has 900 people on a computerized list that he has compiled over the years. Everybody he comes in contact with is on that list. Some of these people will include:

1. Past customers, both buyers and sellers
2. People who came through an open house
3. People who have sent him referrals
4. Attorneys
5. Sales agents who have since left the real estate business (18 percent of Dave's recent sales volume is from this source.)
6. Commercial and industrial salespeople
7. Corporate clients
8. Neighbors
9. Social and recreational contacts

Dave conducts his real estate career by adhering to two fundamental principles, which are:

1. SEE THE PEOPLE
2. KEEP IN TOUCH

To keep in touch, he has devised a three-fold personal promotion program. Every February, everyone on his list receives a *personal production card* which gives the personal sales volume Dave achieved in the previous year. People are attracted to successful people. Your potential customers have no way of knowing how good you are at selling real estate unless and until you tell them. This is why Dave sends a personal production card each year to let his 900 people know just how successful he was in the previous year. The second tool he uses to keep in touch is an annual *Thanksgiving greeting card.* He feels that his most powerful form of personal promotion is his *monthly newsletter.* The newsletter is sent only to those people on the list who still reside in Dave's marketing area. Those living out of town receive the personal card and the Thanksgiving greeting card, but not the newsletter. In the newsletter, he lists his personal production for the three previous years so that the reader is constantly reminded that Dave is a success and someone to be hired to sell a house successfully. His sales since entering the business have been as follows:

1976	$1.1 million
1977	2.2 million
1978	3.4 million
1979	4.1 million
1980	3.5 million
1981	3.5 million
1982	4.4 million
1983	3.5 million
1984	3.5 million

There are two important points to keep in mind when looking at these sales statistics. Dave became a sales manager in 1983, which detracted somewhat from his sales volume. Yet he has been able to take on the demanding challenges of management with minimal loss of sales volume.

He has also managed to maintain a steady volume despite the worst real estate market slump in many years, which occurred in 1981 and 1982. His volume actually increased in 1982 over 1981, which was the opposite of the general real estate trend.

Dave's experience reminds us that this business is a numbers game. If Dave has 900 people who are constantly reminded that he is a winner, he will have a greater chance of reaching his goals than someone with a list of 200 people. It's not enough to be good at what you do. Tell people about your success and tell them often.

The annual production card is Dave's main method of promoting himself, but there are many other ways of promoting yourself and your accomplishments. Forget any false modesty you may have. People want to know who is successful and effective in selling real estate. If you don't put the word out regularly, you are leaving your career to chance: perhaps a greeting card with a handwritten note that you are enjoying a very good year in sales; a personal letter or note to your following, sent out twice a year to keep them informed; a photo of a recent sale, printed on a postcard with the word SOLD stamped on the photo, sent out periodically.

Campaign Strategy 6: *Greeting Cards*

Most people in a sales profession send their customers some kind of greeting card during the traditional Christmas holiday season. Greeting cards of various kinds have been successfully used by real estate salespeople. Some of these include thank-you cards, birthday cards, anniversary cards, and a series of cards that are mailed at the normal holidays for three to five years after a home sale.

A unique approach is to send cards at a time when people are *not* receiving them from anyone else. The following success story is another example of doing something different.

Greeting Card Success Story:
Steven Barnes
Coldwell Banker Realtors
Chicago, Illinois

Do you think you could earn $30,000 in your first year as a real estate salesperson by sending out a few greeting cards? Steve Barnes started doing it in 1972 and continued sending out cards with phenomenal success over an 11-year period.

In 1972, Steve left a seven-year career with Sears Roebuck as national sales promotion manager of work clothing to enter the real estate business with Thorson Realtors, which was subsequently purchased by Coldwell Banker. During Steve's second month in real estate, Steve's father, who was an executive with

Sears, was on a business trip and came across an advertisement in an airline magazine. This ad displayed various greeting cards that were available. Upon returning from his trip, his father showed Steve the ad and suggested that it might be a good idea to use these unique greeting cards as a means of contacting people Steve knew to obtain potential business.

Steve decided to give it a try. He ordered a catalog from the publishing company and bought an original quantity of 200 cards. He was further encouraged to do this by his manager, who told him, "The more people get from you, the less likely they are to forget you."

Steve compiled a mailing list of people who knew him on a first-name basis. He put each name and address on a regular 3″ × 5″ card. He hand addressed each envelope and wrote a personal note on each card asking for referrals. Eventually, this list totaled 100 names, which Steve calls his "magic 100." Each time he received a referral, he made a notation on the 3″ × 5″ card of the referring party. Every six months, he reviewed the file to see who was or was not giving him referrals. If someone was not actively helping him, he sent them cards less frequently than those who were sending referrals. Eventually, his list of 100 people was composed of past customers who were referring him to friends on a regular basis.

Steve began receiving referrals immediately after sending out the original batch of cards. He began getting an average of five or six referrals each month.

Because of his instant success, he decided to mail to his entire list every month. He would select a day in each month that he called his *un*holiday. Because all people respond to humor, he would choose cards that were humorous and send them on days when people did not receive cards from others. He would wish them a happy Labor Day or a happy Fourth of July.

One July, he sent them a Christmas card saying that he wanted to be the first one to wish them a merry Christmas. He received 19 referrals from that one card. In his first year, Steve earned $30,000 in commissions that he could attribute directly to the cards. In his second year, his income climbed to $63,500 and he had 45 transactions that came from the cards.

He always asked for business on an unholiday card. He also sent normal cards on religious holidays and never asked for referrals on those cards because he felt it would be in poor taste to do so. He remembers receiving seven sales from one family because of the constant use of his cards.

Because he had all the business he wanted, he never enlarged his list or followed up his mailings with a phone call, which might have given him more referrals. Steve feels that there were four basic reasons for the success of his card system:

1. He continually noted who was sending referrals so that his list always contained people who were actively helping him on a regular basis.

2. He always hand addressed each envelope and included a personal note so the recipient was treated as a much valued friend.
3. He sent them out each month without fail.
4. His cards were humorous, came at odd times, and always contained a different approach than the usual greeting cards.

Steve used this system for 11 years and says that it was the backbone of his personal strategy for success.

Get a box of 100 index cards and start your own file. Steve's method is easy to do. Don't forget to hand address the envelopes and personally sign each card.

Campaign Strategy 7: *Just-Listed/Just-Sold Cards*

No one is more interested in the neighborhood than the neighbors. The neighbors are interested in everything that happens on their street: new babies; new cars; new house additions; new jobs; and most certainly, new neighbors. Whenever a "for sale" sign goes up, it is the topic of conversation around every neighborhood dinner table that evening.

Probably 90 percent of all salespeople miss this opportunity for instant notoriety by remaining as anonymous as possible. They list the house, provide services to the seller, secure a buyer, and bring the transaction to a successful and sometimes perilous closing without seeking or getting the grateful applause of a watching neighborhood.

There is a little phrase in the real estate business referred to as "Tell 20." This means that when you list a home, you should immediately tell five neighbors to the right, five neighbors to the left, and ten across the street that their neighbor's home is now for sale and that you are representing the seller as the listing agent.

Then when you have a successful sale, you tell the same neighbors that you have become a winner in their midst. Although it would be ideal to do this in person, those few salespeople who communicate with the neighbors do it with a simple just-listed or just-sold card.

This technique can be a powerful part of a personal promotion program because you are communicating with a group of people who have a large investment in the neighborhood and are keenly concerned about home values and salability. Some of these neighbors are contemplating a move and are now considering which listing agent to hire. Your success in their immediate neighborhood could provide you with the winning edge over your competitors.

Just-Listed/Just-Sold Success Story:
Debbie De Grote
Century 21 La Palma, Realtors
La Palma, California

At the age of 23, Debbie De Grote of La Palma, California, will earn more than $300,000 selling real estate. This is no miracle story, but simply another testimony to creativity, good planning, and hard work.

She graduated from high school in June 1979 and received her real estate license in August of that same year. She earned $25,000 between August and December 31, 1979. Her earnings record since reads as follows:

1980	$ 36,000
1981	56,000
1982	108,000
1983	251,000
1984	332,000
1985	427,000

Her sales volume in 1984 was $13 million and $14.3 million in 1985. In 1983, she ranked as the fifth highest Century 21 sales associate in North America in total earnings. She moved to third place in 1984.

Debbie began her career understanding the role she had to play in her own success. She decided to concentrate on two subdivisions, each having 600 homes. Lakewood has homes ranging in price from $95,000 to $110,000 while Cerritos' prices go from $130,000 to $190,000.

As do most top producers, Debbie uses a combination of techniques to promote herself and build her visibility in these two residential areas. Her personal program is made up of four separate and distinct steps:

1. Door-to-door personal calls: Monday, Tuesday, Wednesday, and Thursday are her personal calling days. She goes to *100 homes* on each of these days. She subscribes to a service that provides her with recipe-of-the-month cards, and she gives one of these recipe cards to each homeowner. If there is no one home, she leaves it for them. So if she calls on 100 people per day for four days a week, she

gets to 400 homes a week or 2,000 a month. With a total of 1,200 homes in both subdivisions, Debbie *actually visits each home almost twice a month.* Obviously, she must vary the item she gives the homeowners in order to maintain their interest.

2. Just-listed cards: Each subdivision has 600 homes. Every time she takes a listing in one of the two subdivisions, she has a local printer prepare 600 door hangers with her picture on them. Each door hanger carries the message that she has just listed a new property, giving the property address, her name, office address, and phone number. She then hires two neighborhood boys to hang them on all 600 homes in the area in which the new listing is located. Few sales associates use just-listed cards regularly. Those who do use them send out between 20 and 50 to surrounding homes on the same street as the new listing. Her just-listed program is unique in a number of ways:

   a. They are in the format of a door hanger.

   b. They include her photo.

   c. They are hand delivered.

   d. Every homeowner in the subdivision receives one on each new listing.

3. Just-sold cards: When a listing sells, each homeowner receives a just-sold card prepared in the same manner as the just-listed card. These are also hand carried to each home and placed on the front door of 600 homes.

4. Monthly newsletters: All 1,200 homeowners

receive a monthly newsletter that Debbie purchases from E.C.M. Newsletters of Houston, Texas. These also include her photo, are printed with a four-color process, and provide helpful hints to the homeowner. They are bulk mailed to each home. In the January issue, she inserts a letter thanking the homeowners for their kindnesses, referrals, and business in the preceding year. Later, in the spring, she includes another letter reminding the residents that now is the time to put their home on the market for the active summer season.

Debbie estimates that all 1,200 homeowners receive an average of five to six exposures to her or her promotion materials each month. Could you think of any other real estate salesperson if you were a resident in one of these two subdivisions?

In addition to her geographic-farming program, she is compiling a list of past customers, who receive a monthly newsletter and a personal phone call three times a year. All past customers also receive birthday cards, wedding anniversary cards, and Christmas cards.

Debbie has a full-time secretary who follows up on the myriad of details that are inherent in a marketing effort and sales volume of this magnitude.

You may say to yourself that you cannot and will not call on 100 people a day and do all the other things that Debbie does in such huge quantities.

What will you do? Will you choose an area and:

- Call on 10 people a day?
- Send out 50 just-listed cards around each listing?
- Send out 50 just-sold cards around each sale?
- Mail 200 newsletters a month?

Start doing something regularly. Begin a good habit of prospecting and keep it going.

Campaign Strategy 8: *Newsletters*

An effective promotional tool that has been increasing in popularity is the newsletter. A newsletter accomplishes two important purposes:

1. It provides the reader with information that is intended to benefit him or her directly.
2. It keeps you and your successes in front of a target audience on a regular basis in an unobtrusive manner.

You can produce your own newsletter or purchase a newsletter service from a variety of companies. They both have advantages and disadvantages. Your own design can contain local information that may be pertinent to your target group, either a social or geographic farm. You, of course, have great versatility with your own paper and are free to make changes in content or layout as you see fit. It is also a lot of work gathering the news, writing the copy, taking it to a typesetter, getting it printed, and labeling and mailing.

If you purchase a completed newsletter, it is professional in appearance and may include some photos printed in full color. You may have little or no input regarding its content and the articles may not address the particular interests of your clientele. Typical articles will include recipes, general information on mortgage financing, and ideas on decor and maintenance of a home.

People do enjoy reading these newsletters, and the newsletters have become a valuable medium for communication between salespeople and their constituency. There are some rules of thumb that may be valuable in utilizing the full potential of a newsletter:

1. The content should provide a real service to the reader.
2. It should be easy to read and brief in length.
3. Your photo, name, address, and phone number should be prominently displayed.
4. It should preferably be sent to your target group every month or at least quarterly.
5. You should offer a no-obligation market analysis of the recipient's home in each issue.
6. Every issue should recite some recent success you have had. This will continually impress the reader with the irrefutable fact that you are a winner.
7. The number of newsletters that you should mail will vary depending on your situation. Don't use newsletters unless you are prepared to send out a minimum of 300 and ideally around 1,000.

Proper design and use of a newsletter that is consistently sent on a regular basis can serve as the primary catalyst to launch and sustain a quality image of success and reliability.

Newsletters Success Story:
Sam Fudenberg
Edina Realty
St. Paul, Minnesota

Let's meet Sam Fudenberg of St. Paul, Minnesota. In 1984 Sam sold $6 million in real estate with each home selling in the $85,000 price range. A full 50 percent of this sales volume came from his consistent and creative use of a newsletter.

In 1976 he started out with 200 people whom he identified as friends, acquaintances, and potential customers. He came across an advertisement from a company in Walnut Creek, California, selling a newsletter service. He decided to subscribe to this newsletter service, which is entitled, *Money Talk.*

All the names on Sam's list are members of a social farm that he has continued to develop over the years. The number of names on the list has grown from the original 200 to 1,600. He has added to the list from the following sources:

1. Past customers
2. Class reunion booklets
3. Telephone directories of previous places where he has worked
4. His own acquaintances such as his barber, banker, cleaner, other business contacts, and social and recreational friends.

He mails 1,600 newsletters each quarter to his mailing list, which he is now putting on a computer. Each newsletter is sent in an envelope with an article or two that Sam feels may have some useful and pertinent information for the person receiving it.

He has concluded that this program costs him $1 per name per year. This includes four newsletters, envelopes, stamps, labels, extra articles, and the labor to put it all together.

Sam does not spend a lot of time on this program other than the consistent self-discipline needed to continue adding names and addresses of people he encounters each year. Sam says that this effective yet simple program is the backbone of his entire sales strategy of building a personal following who remember Sam Fudenberg when they think of real estate.

Right for Buying

Timing the purchase of a home involves the tricky business of balancing mortgage interest rates with home prices. When one is up, the other is apt to be down, and vice versa.

On this basis, this is a good time to buy. Although mortgage costs are higher, the rise in housing prices has been squeezed below the rate of inflation.

"While buying a house in 1984 will not be as good as buying one in 1983, the total cost increase will be lower than in many previous years," says John Pfister, vice president and manager of market research for Chicago Title Insurance Co., a major insurer of property titles.

Pfister says his firm's analysis tracks housing costs and mortgage interest rates over a 12-year period dating to 1972. It reveals that, for the period analyzed, there was a trade-off between home prices and the cost of money borrowed to finance the purchase of a home.

"While the correlation isn't perfect, the data shows that when mortgage interest rates have risen in the past, real estate inflation has slowed down. On the other hand, when mortgage rates have been more reasonable (affordable), home prices have escalated more rapidly," Pfister observes.

For example, assume that you bought a house when mortgage interest rates were at or near the high end of the cycle. Your monthly mortgage payment would be higher. But the home you bought probably has greater potential for future appreciation because, most likely, you paid less for it than you would have if interest rates were lower.

The reverse also holds true. If you bought a home when mortgage rates were lower, home costs would be rising more quickly. So, while it cost you less to finance the purchase, you probably paid more for the house. Thus, the potential for future appreciation is less.

Historically, the cost of buying a home has risen annually. In the period between 1972 and 1984, average resale home prices increased 105.4 percent, or 8.78 percent annually.

But home prices are only part of the story. During this period, mortgage rates also trended higher, with the average cost of financing a home rising 71.4 percent over the 12-year period, or an average of 5.95 percent annually.

"When home prices and the cost of borrowing are combined, we find that average home costs rose 176.8 percent, or 14.7 percent annually since 1972," Pfister says.

The increase in home costs were more in some years than others. The peak was 1980, when home prices inflated 11.7 percent and borrowing costs rose 17.6 percent for a combined 29.3 percent increase.

The low point was last year, when home costs rose 3.7 percent while the cost of financing a home declined 16.3 percent.

"From a timing standpoint, the combination of declining mortgage rates and low housing inflation in 1983 produced one of the best times to buy a house in the last 10 years," Pfister says.

"Obviously, if you bought a house 10 years ago, it was cheaper and the mortgage payment was lower than today. But the same also could be said about 20 or 30 years ago. What matters to today's buyers is how the value of a home purchase now will stack up in the future," he believes.

ARM Yourself

REALTORS® are urging borrowers to ask these questions before accepting an adjustable rate mortgage.
• What is the initial (or qualifying) interest rate on the ARM?
• How long is this initial rate in effect? When is the first rate and/or payment adjustment? (Six months? One year?)
• To what index is the ARM's interest rate tied?
• What is the current level of the index?
• How can I (the borrower) use the index and margin to calculate my initial loan interest rate now and at the first adjustment?
• What will happen to my interest rate at the first adjustment, assuming the index rate stays the same? And what monthly payment changes can I expect at that time?
• What is the annual percentage rate of the loan? How does this compare to the APR on other ARMs and a fixed-rate loan?
• How often is the interest rate on the mortgage adjusted? How often does the monthly payment change?
• Is the loan assumable? What are the qualification features? Will the original caps still be in effect? If not, what are the new "caps"?

ALTERNATIVE: Let us ask these questions for you! It's our job to assist you in all areas of your real estate needs.

With mortgage rates again tending to rise, combined housing inflation and higher money costs are expected to increase total home costs by about 18 percent in 1984. While buying this year will not be as good a deal as last year, the total increase will be lower than in many previous years, including 1978 when home resales peaked in the nation.

Pfister likes the present timing for a home purchase because home prices have been climbing at a rate below inflation. This year, home prices are expected to rise about 3.5 percent vs. 5 percent for the Consumer Price Index, which is the standard measure of inflation.

Those buying a home today will be acting at a time in the cycle when real estate prices have been depressed by the high cost of borrowing. However, while mortgage rates in the future are expected to remain high by historical standards, they're not expected to show the sharp increases of the past, he says.

"If borrowing costs over the next 12 years were to rise by the same 71 percent they rose over the past 12 years, we'd be looking at interest in the 25 percent range by 1996. That isn't likely," Pfister believes.

He thinks it's more likely that mortgage rates will stabilize and fluctuate in a range that is well below that level. If this happens, buying a home at today's depressed prices will be seen as a solid investment five to 10 years down the line.

Between 1973 and 1979, home prices inflated 10.1 percent annually while inflation measured by the CPI rose 8.2 percent. Between 1980 and 1984, home prices advanced only 5.5 percent vs. 7.6 percent for the CPI.

"What this means is that housing prices got ahead of themselves in the earlier period and are now rising slower than the cost of other goods and services. Realistically, this can't be expected to go on indefinitely," Pfister says.

"If the cost of money does not continue to spiral higher, at some point home prices can be expected to catch up with the general rate of inflation. Those who buy now should be able to see the value of their homes rise.

"If the buyer can afford the cost of money today, the timing for a home purchase is as good as most years."

Pfister observes that the availability of more flexible mortgage instruments that adjust up or down with the interest rate cycle bolster this reasoning.

"This option is especially attractive if we're anywhere near the high end of the interest rate cycle," he adds.

LET SUN IN

Solar is more than just a passing fad in new home design. Industry analysts say as many as half the new homes built by 1990 will feature sun-storing capabilities. Reason: Passive solar design, although costing about 10 percent more than traditional designs, can sometimes slash heating costs by 50 percent if the homes are constructed properly. Large windows facing the south and fans that push the warm air throughout the home are all it takes. You can also receive partial energy tax credits for the installation.

CHOOSING

The need to engage a professional financial planner is no longer the sole preserve of the rich.

Given that inflation is becoming an acknowledged fact of life and could come roaring back with a vengeance, middle income Americans are finding themselves bumped into higher tax brackets while the purchasing power of their dollars continues to shrink. Growing numbers of them are waking up to the fact that their wealth, whether already held or still being acquired, is under attack. Consequently they seek help from a financial planner.

This growing market has not been overlooked by the various segments of the financial services community. Financial planners seem to be popping up everywhere. Since virtually anyone can call himself a financial planner, consumers must look beyond this title to protect their interests.

Keep in mind accountants, stock and bond sales people, bankers, tax and estate attorneys, real estate and tax shelter salespeople and insurance agents have expertise in narrow, highly specialized areas of the financial services industry, but may not be equipped or inclined to deal with the broad range of topics which must be balanced to develop sound personal financial strategies.

These specialists may all have a part to play in providing financial services, but they are not the proper people to start with for comprehensive financial planning. Given their particular specialties, they quite literally have conflicts of interest in rendering advice. If you want the help of a professional to begin planning for your financial future, should not that expert be able to deal with the broadest range of your financial goals and needs before he begins pitching specific investment alternatives?

Unless a planner displays a willingness to understand a client's personal needs and objectives, what he practices under the guise of financial planning is suspect. If a particular investment is promoted by a financial planner before he has taken into account his client's situation, he cannot be putting that client's interests first. It must be recognized that there is no such thing as the perfect investment, the alternative suited for everyone.

Although the field of financial planning is new and not fully regulated, the profession has sought to regulate itself and establish a credentialing program for its members. The Certified Financial Planner of CFP designation was first granted in 1972 by The College for Financial Planner in the 70s parallels the evolution over 30 years ago in the field of accounting when the CPA planning what the CPA is to accountants, namely the symbol of a higher standard as recognized within the profession. To become a Certified Financial Planner, an individual must demonstrate expertise in six areas which establish his ability to deal with all financially related issues confronting his clients. The CFP designation is your assurance that a planner has a broader range of expertise than your typical stockbroker, insurance agent, REALTOR *, banker or attorney who most often have a myopic point of view.

Just as you approach engaging the services of any professional, whether doctor, lawyer, dentist or CPA, we urge you to shop around for a planner. The purpose of your shopping and interviewing is to find a financial expert whose philosophy and method of doing business are of a standard which will not disrupt your peace of mind. We strongly urge you to seek out a generalist who is capable of analyzing the full range of issues that compromise your total financial picture.

IMPROVEMENTS

For those who are considering a home renovation project, there's a free booklet you might find useful. Titled "Home Improvements . . . An Equation for Increased Value," it offers a system for evaluating how much you'll get in return for your investment. For example, the brochure says the "true cost" for every $10,000 spent on adding a new room, garage or porch enclosure is actually only $4,625. That's because, based on data compiled from a survey of several hundred members of the American Institute of Real Estate Appraisers, the increase in space adds $5,375 to the home's resale value. For every $5,000 spent on energy improvements, the booklet says you can count on recovering about half the cost when you sell. The brochure is free from Alcan Building Products, Box 1100, Warren, OH 44482.

HOME HEAT

Ever wonder what's the cheapest of the traditional residential energy sources? The U.S. Department of Energy just completed a study comparing electricity, natural gas, No. 2 heating oil, propane and kerosene.

In a controlled situation, with the heating unit operating with the same efficiency rating, DOE rated natural gas the least costly. No. 2 heating oil was the second least expensive, followed by kerosene, propane and electricity.

PLANTS

A booklet from Ohio State University offers detailed advice on keeping your houseplants healthy. A discussion of how indoor environmental factors interrelate is supplemented by tables and text explaining how to diagnose and cure plant diseases and the proper pesticides to rid your plants of common insects and other pests.

Pest and Disease Control on Indoor Plants. 19 pp. Publications Office, Ohio State University, Cooperative Extension Service, 2120 Fyffe Rd., Columbus, Ohio 43210. Price: $1.50 plus 54 cents for postage.

I use the newsletter shown on page 134–35. Printed on a monthly basis for seven years, it enabled me to dominate a lucrative residential area in the face of stiff competition. You will notice that the front side was made available to the residents of Lathrup Village for their own personal communications with one another. They would send the blank form in to me with the items they wanted to appear in the paper. The reverse side was dedicated to selling me and my most recent sales successes. I chose this residential community as my constituency. So, my target was a geographic grouping and my campaign to sell myself to this community was a monthly newsletter. At one time I was selling 70 percent of all the homes being sold in this city of more than 6,000 people.

The fundamental decision you have to make regarding newsletters is whether to buy an existing one or write your own. Newsletter services are advertised in the classified section of the *Realtor News*, which is published 39 times per year. This is a product of the National Association of Realtors, headquartered in Chicago, Illinois.

Though it sounds difficult to write your own, it is the most effective because it addresses local issues with a local flavor. You may have a friend with a writing flair who will help you, or you can go to your local college and find a student or faculty member in the journalism department. Where there's a will, there's a way!

The Lathrup Journal ©

Volume 1 Number 4   July, 1971

ECOLOGICALLY SPEAKING...
WE LOOK GREAT!

Under the direction of Mr. and Mrs. Donald Goray, the "Plant-In" at McIntyre School evolved into a huge success. Along with donations, expert gardeners offered suggestions and expert shovelers offered strong backs and together the School blossomed. Thanks goes to Mrs. David Anderson, Joyce Uzelac, Frank Rowland Family, Nancy Bauer, Bruce Benedict Family, Mr. A.G. Lindbery, Mrs. Diane Uyelac, Joseph Elliott Family, Millie Lloyd and children, Warren and Dorothy Boos, Bill Gould, Dan Hittler, Peter Salmon, Neil Jackson, Albert Ripple Family, Ken Cruickshenk, Vaughan Organ Family, Robert Bean Family, Jeannette, Al Pott Family, Frank DeSantis, Mrs. Lewis Dunn, C.J. Lundbert and Jon, Murray Yoller, Mr. and Mrs. Robert Artz and many elementary and junior high children.

NURSERY SCHOOL NEWS

Looking for an excellent nursery school for your four year old? Mrs. Lucena Caster of the Community Nursery of Lathrup announces a new class opening in the fall on MWF afternoons. If you are interested, write Mrs. Caster in care of the Community Congregational Church on Southfield Road.

PARADE POST SCRIPT

Thank you to Bev Clemo and Pat Herrmann and all who contributed to a great parade.

CONGRATULATIONS SERGEANT!

Patrolman Andy Misner has been promoted to Sergeant of the Lathrup Police Department. He has personally headed the Drug Awareness program and we are most appreciative.

PRAYER FOR YOUTH

The young need someone
to listen to them
Lord.
Open my ears that much wider
so that by talking to me
they may be more willing
to listen to You.
Grant them
confidence and guidance
where they have a right
to expect it.
I really want their world
to be better than mine.
Amen

RATS IN LATHRUP?

Theatrically speaking, they'll arrive August 5, 6, and 7, for an appearance in the Lathrup Children's Theater presentation of "Pied Piper of Hamlin," by Bette Butterworth. Almost 100 children are participating both before and behind curtain. The team of Ralph and Joan St. John is responsible for direction and production. The play centers around a town infested with a "chorus of rats" until the arrival of the Pied Piper who "pipes" them away. When the Piper is refused his pay, the trouble really begins! You and your children will enjoy this summer treat. Tickets are $1 available at the door or by calling Mrs. Susick at 358-0681.

TWIN COUNT NEXT MONTH**PROMISE

LOOKING FOR A HELPER?

The following young people have submitted their names to Lathrup residents as job candidates. Please keep this list for reference as it will be published once.

Betsie Beals - 17	557-7471 · babysitting	
Jim Turner - 14	356-4472 grass, odd jobs	
Art Plante - 16	352-8143 odd weekend jobs	
Pam Crawford - 21	356-2267 babysitting at night	no weekends
Jean ne Gadwa - 16	352-3276 babysitting	
Tim Gadwa - 12	352-3276 odd jobs	
Dan Gadwa - 15	352-3276 odd jobs	
Kathy Gleeson - 12	353-9480 babysitting	
Laurie Burgess - 15	557-9140 babysitting	
Katie Yuhas - 16	357-4536 babysitting days	
Ronnie Jono - 13	353-5419 odd jobs	
Gene Capuzzi - 16	356-0099 odd jobs	
Dave Malon - 15	353-8037 baby sitting and odd jobs	
Karen Dorr - 18	358-3911 babysitting	

(P.S. all mentioned they would "dog sit" for vacationing parents.")

HOOTENANY IN LATHRUP?

Yes siree! Pick up a recreation schedule at Lathrup or McIntyre School and get the details teens!

**GREAT
AMERICAN**

BACK CORNER BLOSSOMS

Get your license plates on in time?...a few cars in Lathrup haven't seen light since March 31...we made it this year 8 hours after the deadline...actually the plates (including one for a yellow trail bike) were quite confortable in the buffet drawer...my hero attached them just in time to drive to work April 1...why "expose them to the weather" any sooner than necessary?...by the way,...the bulbs must have turned themselves around 'cause they're comin' up...if there's one thing we're good at around here it's multiplication and growth!   NJE

OUR EDITOR

Tom Ervin

There's something new in Lathrup these days--my sold sign at 27605 Morningside Plaza! Are you thinking of selling your home? Consider my credentials:

1. Membership in not 1 but two multiple listing services.
2. Unique computer service which reveals every home currently for sale and every home sold in the past 12 months.
3. THE LATHRUP JOURNAL which reaches every resident and features your home as shown on this page.
4. BOOK OF HOMES - a magazine printed each month including a photo of your home.
5. A very real commitment by me giving you the most personal and professional representation available today.

WATCH US! CALL US! USE US!
WE'RE MOVIN!
Great American Realty
19080 W. Ten Mile Road
355-0033
We'd love to hear from you -
358-3729

SOLD
ANOTHER
**GREAT
AMERICAN**
HOME FOR SALE
355-0033

S O L D

"A GREAT AMERICAN HOME"

Feeling a little cramped in your home these days? This 4 bedroom custom built Antonelli ranch with 3000 sq. ft. in the Estate Section of Lathrup is just for you. Imagine three fireplaces, a lovely family room, formal dining room, family kitchen with built-ins, 65x15' recreation room, covered terrace, 3 car garage with circular drive and Anderson windows just waiting for your inspection. Call Tom Ervin, 355-0033, for an appointment.

Would you like to see your home here next month? CALL US!

Campaign Strategy 9: *A New Model Open House*

Everyone has heard of the Sunday open house. Yet it is one of the most misunderstood marketing techniques used in the real estate business. Most people think the purpose of an open house is to sell a certain home to whomever may come through on a given Sunday. If no one comes at all, the open house is declared a failure and a waste of time. The real justification for an open house is twofold.

1. To provide a service to the property owner
2. To put you, the salesperson, in a position to promote yourself and thereby gain additional customers

A new home model being offered by a builder provides additional opportunities not available in the typical resale home:

1. Being new, it attracts more potential buyers.
2. The decor and furnishings are usually professionally appointed.
3. Most builders have flexibility regarding selling terms that is not possible in a privately owned residence.
4. If the customer does not like the floor plan or location, both can be addressed by the builder.
5. Builders may offer unique financing packages.
6. The successful sale of a builder's home could lead to repeat business.

Most resale-home salespeople are ill-equipped to represent a new home properly because they are unfamiliar with many of the home's physical and mechanical features. The extra effort necessary to learn all the jargon of new-home sales could enable you to become a much sought after person by the building community.

Working A New-Model-Home Success Story:
Pam McKinnie
Wallace & Wheeler, Inc.
Seattle, Washington

Most real estate salespeople have worked a builder's new-home open house. We usually pick up a few stray lookers who may one day become buyers for some house, but not necessarily the one we are holding open. Pam McKinnie of Seattle makes more than $50,000 a year turning builder open houses into her sole selling technique. Like all other success stories in this book, Pam has taken a simple situation and worked it to perfection. Let's examine her system.

Pam holds open new homes in the $100,000–

$140,000 price range. Her monthly schedule is as follows:

First and third week—both Saturday and Sunday plus two weekdays
Second and fourth week—Saturday or Sunday plus three weekdays

She has found that the best traffic on weekdays is noon to 2 P.M. and after 5 P.M. On Saturday, it is morning and early afternoon. Sundays are best in the afternoon and evening.

Now that she has been doing this for more than four years, she has a well-defined method of turning lookers into customers. While sitting in the model, Pam assumes everyone that comes in is a buyer for this home or another new home. Because the new homes she represents are priced over $100,000, she also assumes that all potential buyers now own a present house and are looking to upgrade to a better one.

When potential buyers enter the model, she shows them around and does some initial qualifying to see if they could afford to purchase a home in this price range. Pam feels that one must work smart by spending time with only those people who will buy within the next six months. Once that has been determined, she tells them that in order to move up they must know the current value of their present house.

After they agree that she must come out to their existing home to determine its value, she always has her appointment book ready to button down the time for her visit. In making the appointment, she tells them that she will not be giving them a price in this first visit. She will be collecting information that will help her arrive at a value. During this first visit, she does ask for their opinion of what they think it is worth. She sets the second appointment with them before she leaves their home.

She lists 40 percent of all homes on the second visit. Once she finds the new home they want, she is successful in listing 80 percent of these buyers.

In four and a half years of selling, Pam has sold every single listing taken within the first 30 days! She accomplishes this through the power of leverage. When the offer is written on the new home, she inserts a clause that makes the purchase of the new home contingent upon the sale of the existing home within 30 days. Some builders will not accept an offer that is contingent upon the sale of a present home. A 30-day contingency, however, is a short one that does not keep the new home off the market long. On the other hand, it is long enough to market the existing home if it is priced properly.

Because the customers know they will lose the new home without a sale on their home within 30 days, Pam is able to get them to price their home to sell. If they balk at pricing their home properly, she will remind them that they will be able to purchase the new home only if they are successful in selling their present home in these critical 30 days.

The biggest problem we have in the real estate

business is getting people to price their property to sell. Pam McKinnie has found a method that gives her tremendous clout to persuade each new home buyer to price his or her home for an expeditious sale.

The next time you are holding a new home open, try Pam's system. It works!

Campaign Strategy 10: *Customer Service*

Because the real estate brokerage business is a service business, you would probably expect that all homeowners and prospective home purchasers receive the same basic quality of service. The facts tell us otherwise. The enormous disparity in the quality of service offered by Realtors is legendary.

Frankly, the majority of homeowners get poor service from their listing agent. Most buyers have very little loyalty to a particular sales associate because they are always searching for that person who will provide the totally professional service that they want.

This situation provides an opportunity for the alert, hard-working salesperson who decides to provide exceptional service and thereby derive a reputation for so doing. No salesperson could ever find a more avid supporter than a satisfied customer.

Customer Service Success Story:
Marge Steineke
First United Realtors
Chicago, Illinois

Marge Steineke has made a success of herself by working only half days in the real estate business. As we all know, each day has 24 hours. Marge works 12 hours a day, 7 days a week. So, you might say that she works 7 half days each week. Hard work is certainly responsible for much of her success.

In her first year, 1982, she sold $1 million in sales volume. In 1983, she did $2.5 million, and in her third year she surpassed the $4 million mark.

This marvelous record began like most do, very

humbly. Although she entered the real estate business with a personal commitment that she would not fail, she almost did. She sold nothing in her first five months. She finally sat down and decided to forget her great career goals and just concentrate on making that first sale.

Marge had two previous work experiences that she was able to use in real estate. She had worked for six years for Illinois Bell Telephone in the customer-service department. She had also been the manager of a 600-unit apartment complex. Both of these jobs taught her the importance of doing all you can to provide good service to the customer.

Let's look at the Marge Steineke method of providing customer service to a seller, a buyer, and a past customer.

Giving Good Service to a Seller.   At the listing presentation, Marge provides the seller with a complete competitive market analysis, including currently listed, expired, sold, and withdrawn properties. She talks about the condition of the seller's house and what should be done to improve its salability, providing a list of craftsmen if the seller would like to get some bids for necessary repairs.

The day after receiving the listing, she sends the seller a handwritten note thanking him or her for the opportunity to sell the property for them. That same day she sends 40 to 50 just-listed cards into the neighborhood and a just-listed card to each cooperating broker who may have a buyer for a home in that area.

When she receives an inquiry from another broker about a specific property, she tells him or her about every other listing that she currently has in that price range.

As an enticement to tour her listings, Marge gives a bottle of wine to each sales associate who tours her properties. She also gives a bottle of wine to those people who come through an open house. Marge believes that you should invest 10 percent of your earnings back into your business in order to build a larger future sales volume.

She prepares her own ad copy for each listing so that the proper features are highlighted in the media.

She also does what all of us should do. She calls each of her sellers each week, even if she does not have any news to report. Marge says that bad news is better than not communicating with them at all.

She is very precise in following up on every detail of the closing process while keeping the seller fully informed of the progress.

As you can see, she puts in a lot of personal effort in promoting the property and keeping the seller informed.

Giving Good Service to a Buyer. When working with out-of-town buyers, Marge sends them a packet filled with information on her area. She takes transferee buyers on an area tour that includes the local schools, library, shopping areas, country clubs, houses of worship, hospitals, and other places of special interest.

At her first meeting with any buyers, she will impress them with the fact that she is genuinely concerned about them and their needs. She says that she will find the ideal home for them but that they must remain loyal to her and not look at homes with other agents. In order to understand their preferences, she asks them to send her a photo of their present home and how they would like to change it.

She always tours in advance every home she is going to show the buyers. She feels that her own credibility will be damaged if she does not check each home before showing it.

She always tries to determine what is important to her buyer in the area of financing such as a quick closing, good service, or the most favorable interest rate. Answers to these questions help her decide which lender to recommend.

Marge also maintains a complete file of information that she gives her buyers so that they may become better oriented to the community. These items include booklets published by the various cities in the area, newsclippings, community-theater information, bus and train schedules, names and phone numbers of people to contact in such organizations as a newcomers' club, women's club, or garden club.

If a buyer is male and has a spouse who is a homemaker or if a single woman who is a homemaker is a buyer, Marge throws a coffee party for the homemaker, takes her shopping, or introduces her at lunch to someone she thinks could become her friend.

As in serving a seller, Marge is willing to do more than the average salesperson in order to get results and maintain the loyalty of the customer.

Serving the Past Customer. Marge tries to keep in touch with her past customers in a meaningful way by using the personal approach. She gives all her buyers a unique gift after they have moved into their new homes. As an example, a recent customer was interested in horses, so Marge gave her a pewter statue of a horse.

If a young couple have bought their first home, Marge gives them a free dinner on her American Express Card. She buys 200 Christmas wreaths from the Boy Scouts, which she personally delivers to her past customers. If someone has given her a referral during the previous quarters, he or she will receive a lovely centerpiece for the dining-room table. She sends birthday cards and anniversary cards marking the anniversary of the buyers' moving into their new home. She also sends 200 Christmas cards. She brings a pot of hot coffee over to the new home on the day her buyers are moving in. If she hears that a past customer is ill, she sends a bouquet of flowers and her best wishes for a speedy recovery.

Marge obviously invests lots of attention, time, and money in all her customers and clients, both present and past. This total commitment to service has enabled her to double her sales volume each year in her first three years.

As with other stories herein, Marge seems like a wonder woman. Just pick out two or three of her ideas that you like and build them into your regular routine.

Go back through the story and put a check mark next to the ideas you want to do, or better yet, write them down and tape them to the inside cover of your daily calendar so you won't forget.

Campaign Strategy 11: *Getting Listings by Working with Buyers*

Most of the strategies mentioned in this book are designed to help you attain a large inventory of listings through the use of an imaginative approach to potential sellers. The technique that we are about to discuss enables you to build listings through the successful servicing of buyers' needs. If you do a conscientious job in helping a buyer purchase a home, that same person will refer you to others and seek you out when the time comes to sell. Most buyers feel, and rightly so, that no one is more qualified to sell their home than the person who sold them their home originally. This technique is particularly successful in a high-transferee area.

Getting Listings by Working with Buyers Success Story:
Ann MacDonald
Real Estate One, Inc.
Detroit, Michigan

Meet a $50-million grandmother. Ann MacDonald of Detroit, Michigan, is rewriting real estate history with a unique selling style of service and perseverance.

In her 12 years in the real estate business, she has sold $59,218,458 in sales volume in a market that has an average price of $80,000 per transaction. Her sales history is as follows:

1974	$ 510,388
1975	1,176,485
1976	2,438,675
1977	4,345,682
1978	6,055,840
1979	6,578,304
1980	4,609,132
1981	6,090,755
1982	4,652,220
1983	7,067,813
1984	6,908,350
1985	8,784,814

Besides being a lover of people, Ann is also a great friend to animals. As early as she could drive a car, she began carrying cat food and dog food in the trunk of her car for any stray animals she might encounter.

Actually, her love of cats indirectly led her into the real estate business. In 1974, at the age of 56, Ann was enjoying her life as a homemaker when her Siamese cat suddenly died. Because Ann was fond of the cat, she became anxious to get out of the house and do something that would take her mind off the loss of her pet. She noticed in the evening paper that Real Estate One was having a career night in a neighboring community. She went to the meeting and left a $65 deposit for a prelicense class. Upon graduating from the class and obtaining her license, she called the woman who had recruited her and told her that although she had her license she had decided not to go into real estate. The office manager asked her if she could come in that afternoon and help her answer the phone because she was shorthanded in the office. Ann agreed and had a couple call who needed help in finding a house. Ann went out with them and found that she really enjoyed working to help people find the right home. Now, 12 years and 745 sales later, at the age of 68, she still loves helping people find the right house.

What is her system? Ann spends 70 percent of her time working with her buyers and 30 percent with her sellers. She has never solicited a listing directly. She doesn't call on for-sale-by-owner or expired listings. Yet she always carries an average inventory of more than 60 listings at any one time. Every listing she has ever taken has been a referral from a happy previous customer.

She keeps a book of the names, addresses, and phone numbers of people currently looking for a home. When she sees a listing they might like, she makes a copy of the information and mails it to her customer. If the customer is a transferee, she makes up a package of information that will include photos of homes in the buyer's price range, maps, a home-photo book, and Chamber of Commerce data.

Ann believes you have to spend money in order to make it. When she is out showing property, she buys lunch or dinner for her customers. If customers purchase a home in the $125,000 price range or higher, she will send them a case of liquor as a house-warming gift. She buys gifts for those who send her referrals. This past Christmas, she bought $500 worth of flowers.

Like all top producers, she spends long hours at her work, from 9:00 A.M. to 10:00 P.M. seven days a week. From time to time, she will take a couple of days off to catch her breath.

She feels that her age has been an asset to her. Most of her customers are much younger than she, and they rely on her for advice and counsel. She has earned this trust because she is honest with her customers about the pros and cons of the many decisions they must make.

Because all her listings are referrals, she makes it clear that she will not take a listing for less than six months. If people do list with her, however, she advertises the listing personally in addition to the ads run by her company.

Despite the lack of any formal sales training and despite her venturing into a new career at the age of 56, Ann MacDonald is proof that everything is possible if you believe in yourself and like what you are doing.

Campaign Strategy 12: *Holiday Activities*

They say that all humans are a drop of intellect in a sea of emotion. This is abundantly true during a holiday season. It is also true that everyone enjoys receiving a gift. Many real estate salespeople win the hearts and minds of potential customers with a kind gesture at holiday time.

Different techniques are employed. Some sales associates call or visit past and potential customers merely to tell them that they are thinking of them during the holidays. Others send appropriate cards for the occasion. Still others give gifts, both simple and elaborate.

All of these efforts are effective and go a long way toward the establishment of a strong emotional bond between you and your clientele. The tangible dividends are future referrals and repeat customers.

Some of the holidays used successfully by real estate sales associates have been Easter (flowers), Halloween (pumpkins, complimentary pictures of the kids in costume), Thanksgiving (a turkey), and Christmas (gifts, cards, flowers, a bottle of wine or champagne).

Holiday Activities Success Story:
Darlene Dipo
Eagar and Company
Salt Lake City, Utah

Meet a very creative and energetic young woman! Darlene Dipo of Salt Lake City, Utah, has innovative ideas that give her a lot of fun and enjoyment in the real estate business and a hefty sales volume of more than $4 million a year. She does all this while taking off Saturday afternoon and all of Sunday each week to be with her family.

We all learned a long time ago that every one of us enjoys receiving gifts from someone who is thinking of us. Darlene has turned this basic truth into a multi-million-dollar real estate sales program.

Some of us in sales remember our past or present customers with a holiday greeting card. Most of us don't even do that much. Darlene has a basic belief that a successful real estate salesperson should plan on investing 10 percent of his or her annual earnings on career-building techniques. She feels that this kind of financial commitment is necessary in order to sustain the loyalty of her present customers and build the future with new ones.

How many of us remember our customers at Easter? Darlene has been going to her local florist for the last 5 years at Easter time to remember 75 to 100 important people in a special way. These people are primarily past customers and others who have referred business to her in the past. She simply asks the florist for 100 of the little white envelopes that you usually include when sending flowers. She takes these home and addresses them to her 100 people. They happen to be the perfect size for her business card, which she encloses in each envelope. After addressing all of them, she returns them to the florist and pays him or her to send these envelopes and an Easter lily to each person. She always receives three to four immediate listings and, of course, many thanks by phone and mail.

Sometime prior to Christmas each year, she gets out the Spiegel catalog and looks for some classy gift item that will be very visible in the home. She has been doing this for the last five Christmas seasons, and it usually takes her most of the month of December. Here is a list of the gifts given in the years 1980–1984:

1980—brass candlesticks
1981—beautiful bouquets of artificial flowers
1982—brass bookends
1983—mahogany wooden ducks with brass beaks
1984—wooden Christmas sleighs

In 1984 she increased the number of recipients of her Christmas gifts to an all-time high of 200 people. By delivering the gifts in person, she is able to strengthen relationships and pick up additional leads for business. The gift is always a quality item so it is much appreciated and placed in a visible part of the home. Each time they see it throughout the year, people are reminded of Darlene and her personal touch in building a strong and lasting friendship.

After each sale, Darlene orders a quality doormat with the new homeowner's name on it. In a couple of weeks, after it is made up, she brings it in person to present to the homeowner. This gives her another opportunity to build those personal bonds of loyalty and a sense of indebtedness to her.

Darlene works hard but she also works smart. Consider a gift-giving program as part of your sales plan.

If you would like to begin a gift-giving program with your valuable customers, start looking early. Darlene uses the Spiegel catalog. Get this and other catalogs and talk to local merchants to see what they suggest.

How much can you spend? Be sure the gift denotes quality and good taste or don't do it.

Make a list and see how many gifts you will need. You should probably begin planning in October so that you can place your order long before the post-Thanksgiving-day shopping rush.

Don't mail the gifts. Deliver them in person so that you can build those bonds of friendship and loyalty stronger each year.

What Does This Mean to Me?

9

The purpose of this book is not only to entertain or inform. As stated in the preface, our purpose is to effect a change in you and the way you approach your real estate career. In order to do that, this final chapter will attempt to relate the lessons learned to your individual situation. Please take out a pen or pencil and let us proceed.

At the conclusion of Chapter 1, we said that every top achiever has

1. a tremendous personal commitment to success;
2. a plan of action.

> **Personal Question 1:** After reading this book, do you believe that real estate sales success is possible for you?

> **Personal Question 2:** Will you commit yourself to implementing an action plan that is right for you?

If the answers to questions 1 and 2 above are yes, then let us continue. If the answer is no to either or both questions, take some time to re-examine the rea-

158

sons. Ultimate success in your sales career must begin with a belief that it is possible. Once believed, success can only be achieved with a plan.

Before exploring your personal strategy, there are some other topics that must be discussed.

Personal Question 3: Do you have a high energy level: If no, why not?

- Is your diet improper?
- Do you get inadequate exercise?
- Are there any other health-related problems?

All top producers have a lot of energy. They cover a lot of ground in a day's time. If Dee Amsler is going to do $7 million a year in volume with an $85,000 average price, that is 80 houses to list, 80 to sell, and 80 to close, plus all the communications with buyers, sellers, and other agents. If your energy level needs improving, do something about it. You will not be able to initiate and sustain a high sales volume without expending a lot of energy.

Personal Question 4: Are you good at dealing with fear?

In any sales position, you are always confronted with new situations. This is also true of real estate sales. All top producers have fears. All top producers deal with them effectively. Three fears usually predominate.

1. *Fear of the Unknown.* Salespeople are always in the presence of strangers and new situations. No two days are alike in the selling business. Of course, new people and new situations provide the variety that is stimulating and rewarding. Nevertheless, some new problems must be faced in which the outcome is uncertain.

2. *Fear of Rejection.* You must be able to deal with the word "No." Not everyone will like you. Some people will choose to do business with someone other than you. All top producers have been rejected in favor of someone else many times.

3. *Fear of Failure.* To be successful in real estate sales, you must be willing to take risks. Inherent in every risk is the chance that you will succeed or fail. Top producers have had their share of failures along the way.

Failure is not in the falling down, but in falling and failing to get back up again. Some of the sales approaches others tried have worked and some have failed. Through this trial and error method, they learned more about themselves and what they could do well. Don't be afraid to take risks. The old saying tells us, "Nothing ventured, nothing gained." Stretch yourself. Try new ideas and learn, learn, learn. The road to success is sometimes strewn with little, temporary failures.

When you were very young, you had many fears. These probably included the fear of riding a two-wheel bicycle. How did you overcome this fear? One day you got on a bike and found it wasn't so bad after all. The same thing applies to a selling situation. Once you do what you were afraid of doing, you are no longer afraid of it.

Actually, overcoming fears is a helpful process because it builds self-confidence to try new ideas. If you have not been very successful in dealing with fears in your past life, now is the time to start.

Personal Question 5: Do you enjoy competing with others?

All top producers thrive on competition. They like winning. They enjoy being chosen to list a home after beating out two other competitors who were also being considered. Top producers always view situations from a competitive point of view. To some people, competition is a dirty word. How do you feel about earning a living through your ability to compete? I hear people say they want to sell real estate because they like people and houses. That's fine, but it is not enough motivation to make it to the top. This is an extremely competitive business, and you have got to clarify your feelings about your *need* to compete.

Personal Question 6: Do you feel comfortable promoting yourself and your successes?

Top producers are not shy. This is not to say that they are offensive or brash. They learned early on, however, that you have to beat your own drum because no one else will do it for you.

I believe women, particularly, feel uncomfortable promoting themselves to the public. Many real estate saleswomen have told me that they have not been raised to brag about themselves or their achievements. I respect that and understand their background. If you consider the success stories mentioned in the previous chapter, however, those women had a very effective way of gaining visibility in their local communities.

Your friends and customers are not mind readers. They can't tell how successful you are unless you keep them informed on the progress of your career in sales. People like to be around winners. Let them know about your victories.

Personal Question 7: Are you willing to invest in your career?

Top producers put a portion of their earnings back into their business. Sam Fudenberg puts out a newsletter. Debbie DeGrote sends out 600 "just-listed/just-sold" cards around every listing. Dee Amsler hires a secretary, rents a computer, and pays for birthday parties. Elly Engberg purchases custom-designed personal brochures. Dave Wilcox pays for a monthly newsletter, a large mailing each February, and Thanksgiving Day greeting cards. Darlene Dipo buys tasteful gifts. Steve Barnes sends out greeting cards. Marge Steineke sends just-listed cards and purchases a variety of gifts. They all spend money in different ways. Their purpose is to build future sales.

Many salespeople don't seem to understand this basic fact. You must spend money to make more money. Sometimes, you have to spend money *before* you begin making sales. Don't be shortsighted. Look not at today but to your future. The $200 you spend today could enable you to earn $2,000 or more in the future.

Personal Question 8: Have you considered the need to have an

ADVANTAGE OVER YOUR COMPETITION?

Every top producer either has or creates an advantage over the competing salespeople in his or her area. Compete with an advantage that will give you a greater percentage of wins than the average salesperson has. Let's look at some of our success stories in the previous chapter to see the advantage they use.

Name	Typical Salesperson	The Advantage
Dee Amsler (Geographic farming)	Call on the phone Send mail	Door to door Her own newsletter Gave out cookbooks Started civic group
Tom Ervin (For sale by owners)	Call on phone Send letter	Sent four postcards Went to door on the fifth day Came back weekly

Eric Olson (Expired listings)	Call on phone Send mail	Made résumé Included photo Sent to absentee owners
Madeline Hayes (Expired listings)	Call on phone	Selected 10 best target listings Previews each one Meets each owner Checks daily
Elly Engberg (Personal promotion)	Business card	Personal brochure Photo included Testimonials Her qualifications
Dave Wilcox	Nothing	Computer mailing Annual production card

USING THE COMPUTER TO GAIN AN ADVANTAGE

Another advantage you can have over your competition is the creative use of a personal computer. This tool has great promise for the aggressive sales associate. Let's look at how Dee Amsler of H.E.R. Realtors uses her computer.

Dee has been using her computer for only a year. As in everything else she does, she has been creative in finding good computer applications that help her directly in gaining the competitive edge in her marketplace.

She now has 150 different form letters on the computer. Any of these letters can be individually retrieved and put up on the computer screen. Each letter can then be addressed to a different person and specific details about this person can be inserted in blanks that are left throughout the letter. After the blanks are filled in, the computer is instructed to print the letter and address an envelope. Some of these 150 letters include the following:

1. A for-sale-by-owner letter.
2. An other-broker expired-listing letter.
3. A thank-you letter to an attorney who attended a recent closing.
4. A thank-you letter to the loan officers who represented the lending institution at a recent closing.
5. A thank-you letter to anyone who gave her a referral.
6. A letter to all owners of two-story homes in her farm when she has a buyer for a two-story home.
7. A weekly letter to the owners of all of her listings that keeps them informed about her efforts.
8. A cover letter with each listing presentation that addresses the pertinent aspects of the subject property.
9. A personal-profile letter that gives her professional qualifications.
10. After the sale agreement has been signed, a letter to the seller telling him or her where the buyer has applied for financing, prospective date for closing, and request for existing title policy.

11. If appropriate, notification that a termite inspection will be performed on the home and request to notify Dee when it is done.
12. Many personal notes prepared and printed on personalized stationery.

In addition to its letter-writing assistance, the computer is also used to keep large, meticulous files on a variety of topics. Some of the filing applications are:

1. All of the homes in her three target subdivisions are categorized by number of stories. When she wants a list of all one-story homes, she can have them appear on the computer screen with the name and address of each owner.
2. A lengthy fact sheet is maintained on each current listing.
3. A client list is kept on all past customers, which has name, address, birthdays, spouse's name, spouse's employer, name of children. When talking to a client by phone, Dee has the client information put on the screen so that all personal data is right in front of her.
4. With the names, addresses, and phone numbers of every home in her three subdivisions, the computer sorts them by last name and prints a telephone directory. Dee now provides, in an attractive $3 red-and-white binder, a directory for all 1,150 homeowners. She also records all changes in this file so that an accurate directory is printed in each subdivision after every 20 to 30 moves.

5. Comparable sales are loaded into the computer for appraisal purposes. When she is in a competitive battle for a listing, Dee invites the homeowner to her office. She lets the homeowner see the comparable information on the computer screen, which makes her opinion of value credible and her listing presentation more professional and convincing than the competition's.

Personal computers can also enable you to do other things. Consider the potential of some of the following ideas:

1. Prepare a visual graph on your personal statistics and those of your market.
2. Print just-listed/just-sold cards with specific information on the subject house. You could purchase continuous forms that have your photo preprinted on one side, allowing the computer to print your message on the reverse side.
3. Print continuous-form open-house announcement cards to be sent through the neighborhood in advance of an open house.
4. Automatically address envelopes and/or postcards to members of your social or geographic farm.
5. Do your personal bookkeeping.
6. Help you follow closing details on your pending sales.

Consider the use of a personal computer as part of your strategy to have the edge over your competition.

YOUR PLAN OF ACTION

Now that you have answered some important personal questions about yourself, let's address the basic ingredients of your plan.

Your Goal. Most top salespeople identify their personal goal in one of four ways:

1. *Earnings Goal.* They decide on the amount of earnings that they want to make in a calendar year. (I want to make $40,000 in 1985.)
2. *Volume Goal.* They pick out a certain sales volume that they want to attain in a calendar year. (I want to sell $3 million in volume this year.)
3. *Ranking Goal.* They want to have a certain position in their peer group because this relates to volume or earnings. (I want to be the top person in my office this year.)
4. *Material Goal.* They have identified a specific thing they want to purchase with their income from real estate sales. (I want to pay for my daughter's college education or for a second home.)

Have you identified specific goals for yourself?

The Best Strategy for You. Our top producers probably chose their strategy through trial and error. Having read their stories, however, you are more informed than they because you can learn from all of their experiences.

Before we examine each strategy to enable you to set your course, we must differentiate between those strategies that produce quick results and those that give long-lasting benefits.

Most people need to create an immediate income while laying the groundwork for a long, successful career. In other words, "Let's make money today so we can still be around tomorrow." Many aspiring salespeople make a fundamental error in choosing a strategy that does not deliver immediate results. They run out of money and/or patience before they begin to reap the rewards of their efforts. Others take care of present income needs but never plant the seeds from their current successes for long-term referrals and repeat business. The ideal combination for you is to choose one short-term and one long-term strategy and implement them simultaneously.

As a beginning sales associate, I chose the short-term strategy of the for-sale-by-owner program described earlier. At the same time, as a long-term strategy, I began developing a 1,400-home geographic farm with *The Lathrup Journal* newsletter shown in campaign strategy 8. I began earning income with the listings I obtained from the for-sale-by-owner program, and I built my visibility and desirability in the geographic farm with the monthly newsletter. This combination of short-term and long-term techniques got me started and kept me going.

Short-Term Strategies (Choose one):

1. For sale by owners
2. Expired listings of other brokers
3. Builder-model home program
4. Good old-fashioned service
5. Getting listings by working with buyers

Long-Term Strategies (Choose one):

1. Social farming
2. Geographic farming
3. Personal canvassing
4. Personal brochure
5. Personal promotion
6. Greeting cards
7. Just-listed/just-sold cards
8. Newsletters
9. Holiday activities
   NOTE: If you are going to work a social or geo-graphic farm, please refer to the pages in the previous chapter where the factors to consider in choosing the right farm are discussed.

Implementation Plan. Unless you schedule your time properly, you will not be able to implement a short- and long-term plan with enough consistency. I have found that the use of a simple calendar can help you plan your month so that you can address each facet of your personal success program. As a guide, I have filled out a sample one-month calendar that I

MARCH   1985

SUNDAY	MONDAY	TUESDAY	WEDNESDAY	THURSDAY	FRIDAY	SATURDAY
					1	2
3	4 Send febo post cards 7pm febo	Sales Meeting 5 Send febo post cards 7pm febo	6 Send febo post cards 7pm febo	7 Send febo post cards take pictures for newsletter 7pm febo	8	9
10	11 Send febo post cards take newsletter to typesetter 7pm febo	Sales Meeting 12 Send febo post cards 7 pm febo	13 Send febo post cards take newsletter to printer 7 pm febo	14 Send febo post cards 7pm febo	15	16
17	18 Send febo post cards address all newsletters 7 pm febo	Sales Meeting 19 Send febo post cards take newsletter to post office 7 pm febo	20 Send febo post cards 7 pm febo	21 Send febo post office 7 pm febo	22	23
24	25 Send febo post cards 7pm febo	Sales Meeting 26 send febo post cards 7pm febo	27 Send febo post cards 7 p.m febo	28 Send febo post cards 7 p.m febo	29	30
31						

used as a sales associate. You will note that it includes other necessary things that must be anticipated in a normal month. Get a calendar that shows a month at a glance and lay out your new program on it.

Monitor and Decide. It is very important to monitor your progress in implementation. For this purpose, I have included a blank and a sample activity chart for you to use. If the results are good, stick with it. If the results are not good, either the strategy is wrong for you or you are implementing it ineffectively. If the short-term strategy is wrong for you, choose another short-term strategy. If the long-term strategy is wrong for you, choose another long-term strategy. Remember, however, that it will take longer for a long-term strategy to show results. It may be the right long-term plan for you and you may be implementing it well. Don't quit before you have given it adequate time to produce for you.

Where have we been in our travels through this book?

We learned the value of doing something your competitor is not willing to do and of providing a unique service to your customer.

We became aware of the three stages in every selling career: prospecting, consolidation, and the reward stage.

People are attracted to winners, and self-made winners have a clear vision of themselves as a success and they have a commitment to make that vision a reality.

An examination of yourself and your salability will enable you to increase your strengths and improve upon your weaknesses. Regardless of your present standing, don't relinquish your rightful place at the top. Go for it!